This Book belongs to the:

ILLINI COUNTRY STITCHERS

LET'S MAKE MORE PATCHWORK QUILTS

By Jessie MacDonald

With 40 Quilt Block Designs

Farm Journal, Inc.
Philadelphia, Pennsylvania

Distributed to the trade by
Doubleday & Company, Inc.
Garden City, New York

OTHER FARM JOURNAL CRAFT BOOKS

Let's Make a Patchwork Quilt

Soft Toys to Stitch and Stuff

Patterns for Appliqué and Pieced Work

Knit Sweaters the Easy Way

Scrap Saver's Stitchery Book

More Scrap Saver's Stitchery

Farm Journal's Homespun Christmas

Farm Journal's Design-and-Sew Children's Clothes

Easy Sewing with Knits

Modern Patchwork

My thanks to students and friends who encouraged me to write this book. Thanks also to Linda White, who quilted the Glittering Star quilt; to Ruth Ballinger, who quilted the Heavenly Bears crib quilt; to Barbara Pharazyn, who typed the manuscript; and to my editor, Jean Gillies, who helped with the writing, the art work and some of the original designs.—J.M.

Book design: Michael P. Durning
Photography: George Faraghan Studio
Illustrations: Len Epstein

Library of Congress Cataloging in Publication Data

MacDonald, Jessie.
  Let's make more patchwork quilts.

  Includes index.
  1. Quilting.   2. Patchwork.   I. Title.
TT835.M263   1984   746.9'7   84-45027
ISBN 0-385-19504-4

Printed in the United States of America

Contents

Introduction

It has been wonderful to see the revival of patchwork and quilting in today's world. I remember sleeping under quilts (sometimes lumpy ones) as a child, picking out favorite patches and enjoying the warmth on cold winter nights. Those quilts were made out of necessity and used daily, so most of them just wore out and disappeared. They remain, for me, only in memories. It is a lucky person who has inherited a homemade family quilt that is still intact.

I've been swept along with the new quilt movement, making quilts for my family and introducing others to the craft through my classes. This time, however, the quilts are for decoration instead of utility. And there is greater appreciation of the homemade quality.

Most of my large quilts are samplers. I prefer samplers because I can combine pieced work and appliqué, mixing a variety of techniques to keep the work interesting. I always begin with traditional patterns, but I often rearrange a few blocks and create some new ones before I'm finished.

My most recent samplers are based on themes, such as birds or Christmas. The Wedding Sampler, for example, has blocks with names like Love-in-a-Mist and Steps to the Altar, along with a sprinkling of hearts.

For this book, I've included a mix of projects—large quilts (including three samplers), crib quilts and a few wall hangings. So you have a wide choice.

You can copy my designs and colors exactly, or you can use my patterns as a beginning for your individual creations. Change the colors or rearrange the designs to suit yourself. If you like a particular block in a sampler, you might decide to make a whole quilt of that one pattern.

Quilt-making has become a happy hobby for many people— so come join us. Once you get a project underway, you won't be counting the hours it takes. You'll be enjoying the work, turning it into a true labor of love.

—Jessie MacDonald

1 Hints and Tips for Piecing and Appliqué

This chapter covers the basic techniques you'll need to make any quilt top in this book. If you're a beginner, use it as a manual and refer to it often. If you're an experienced quilter, I hope you find it a helpful reference.

A first project in quilting ought to be relatively simple. In my classes, I've seen people with no experience tackle the Christmas quilt—and conquer it. (Of course, I was there.) However, if you're brand new to quilting, you might like to begin with something smaller and easier. I'd suggest the Checkerboard and School-house wall hanging on page 137, or the Lady Jane (or Fishing Boy) crib quilt on page 123.

Tools and supplies

These are most of the items you will need to make your work go smoothly.

• *Pins.* I prefer small flexible pins with round, colorful heads that are easy to see. T-pins are handy when stacking layers for basting.
• *Needles.* Use Sharps for basting. These all-purpose needles can make long stitches.

Quilting needles (also called Betweens) are needed for quilting. These are short and help you make nice, short stitches. Start with size 8, then graduate to the smaller size 10. Use quilting needles also for hand piecing and for appliqué.

Crewel or embroidery needles have long eyes to handle floss for embroidery.
• *Thread.* Regular mercerized cotton or cotton-wrapped polyester thread in white is good for hand basting. Use white or a blending color for machine piecing. Choose a matching color for appliqué work.

Use quilting thread in your choice of color for quilting. It's strong and has a coating so it won't tangle easily.

Embroidery floss, which comes in six-strand lengths, is needed for some projects.
• *Thimble.* You may want one for handwork. A thimble will be necessary if you plan to quilt on a frame or with a hoop.
• *Shears.* Keep one pair for cutting paper, poster board or plastic (for templates) and another pair for cutting fabric. (Paper and plastic will dull your good shears.)
• *Embroidery scissors* are handy for close clipping.
• *Ruler and yardstick.* The ruler can be metal, wood or plastic, but use the same one for all measuring. There may be some variation among inexpensive ones.
• *Pencils.* A soft No. 2 pencil, well-sharpened, is fine for general use and for tracing templates on light-colored fabrics. Use a hard No. 5H or 6H pencil to mark quilting lines on light-colored fabrics. You'll also need a yellow, white or silver drawing pencil to mark dark fabrics.
• *Poster board or plastic* is good for making templates (cut-out patterns for tracing shapes on-to fabric) and for transferring quilting or other design lines to fabric. Plastic for this purpose is available in craft stores, and you also can use lids from cof-fee cans and other containers.
• *Fine sandpaper* (optional). To keep fabric from slipping when you're tracing around tem-plates, you can slip a sheet of sandpaper, face up, under the fabric.
• *Dressmaker's carbon paper* in white or yellow is handy for transferring patterns to dark fabric. I use a dry ball-point pen (one with no more ink) with dressmaker's carbon. The rounded tip gives a good line and doesn't tear the paper.
• *Regular carbon paper* is helpful for transferring patterns to poster board.
• *Odds and ends.* Some proj-ects may call for other tools, such as masking tape, felt-tip pen or a compass.

Choosing fabric

One hundred percent cotton is the choice of most quilters, both for the quilt top and the backing. It's easy to handle and to finger-press. However, many present-day quilters mix cottons with cotton/polyester blends, mainly to get a wider choice of colors and prints. I have combined all-cottons with blends and have been pleased with the results. So when someone finds a blended fabric in a print that is just perfect for her needs, I say, "Go ahead and buy it."

If you use washable fabrics and plan to wash your finished quilt, you should prewash and press all the fabrics before you use them. (Also eliminate any that you find are not colorfast.) On the other hand, if you plan to send your finished quilt to the dry cleaners (and I admit I often do this), you may want to omit the prewashing step.

The middle layer of your quilt will be batting, which is sold in rolls of various sizes. I recommend using bonded polyester batting. The bonded surface makes it easy to handle and helps keep the batting in place.

Combining colors

Deciding on colors seems to be the biggest challenge for most quilters. I try to begin with three fabrics, usually prints, that look good together. I choose three values—a light, a medium and a dark. Then I add prints and solids that blend, always keeping a mix of light, medium and dark values.

In selecting prints, I like to have a few medium or large designs as well as some very small ones. When I choose solids, I often include an off-white muslin color.

For most quilts in this book, the number of different fabrics is up to you. There is a minimum number of fabrics needed to complete each block design, but you can repeat the same colors from block to block as you choose.

I tend to assemble a wide variety of fabrics, ranging from four in the Christmas quilt all the way up to an astounding 154 in the Scrap Basket quilt (where most of the pieces were actually small scraps).

People are going to view your quilt from a distance, so try to look at fabrics that way. As you shop, line up several bolts of fabric that you like, then step back to see how they look. When you go to a store, take along swatches of any fabrics you've already chosen. Place the swatches on any new bolt you are considering and see if you like the combination—once again, judging the effect from a distance.

To help you begin your fabric selections, decide on the main color—maybe blue. Look over all the blue prints in the store, and try to find three that go together—one light, one medium and one dark.

Study these prints to see if a second color stands out. Maybe one print has a dusty rose pattern. You now have a clue for adding fabrics. Proceed to check prints in rose tones, adding one or more that blend with your blue choices. Add any solid colors in the same way.

After I have assembled a variety of fabrics, I lay them on the floor in front of the TV set. As I sew (on something else) and watch a program, I glance at the array of fabrics, rearranging, adding and subtracting until I get a mixture I like. If the quilt is to have sashing, I try to decide very early what color it will be and whether it should be a print or solid.

You can keep adding fabrics even after you begin work on the quilt. However, for borders, sashing or backing, do buy all the yardage you need at one time. Fabric from different bolts may vary in color.

Making templates

Templates are cut-out patterns used to trace shapes onto fabric. They should be made of durable material, such as poster board or plastic.

If you use poster board, first copy the pattern onto tracing paper. Then transfer the pattern to poster board by placing a sheet of regular carbon paper between the layers.

The sheets of plastic available in craft shops are easy to use. You can place them directly over patterns in the book and mark them with a special permanent-marking pencil or pen.

Be as accurate as you can in marking and cutting templates. If they are exact, your finished blocks have a better chance of being accurate, too. Label each template with the name of the block and any individual letter or name given that particular piece. Keep sets of templates for each block in a plastic bag or brown envelope so they won't get mixed up.

Most of the quilts in this book have full-size patterns that you can trace directly from the book. You will need to draft templates for only a few large pieces (a 3x15" rectangle, for example). Measure these carefully on your template material, mark and cut out.

To mark long border pieces, I usually cut a template that is as wide as the border and 12" to 15" long. When tracing it on fabric, I keep moving the template along until I have the border length needed.

General piecing

Piecing is done by stitching one piece of fabric to another, either by hand or machine. To piece a block, first assemble all the templates and fabrics you will need for that block.

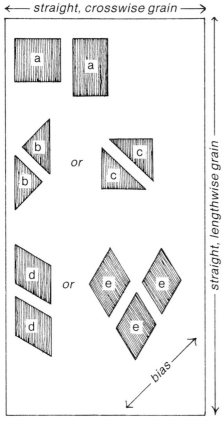

Fig. 1 Positioning templates

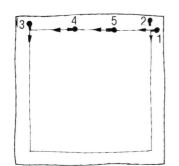

Fig. 2 Pin-basting

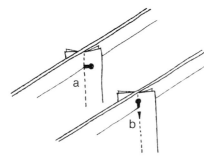

Fig. 3 Pin-basting to match seam lines

Position templates

Place each template, face down, on the wrong side of the fabric, making sure grain lines are correct. (A solid color fabric in a plain weave may be the same on both sides, so either side can be the "wrong" side.)

Looking at Fig. 1, you will see that straight grain runs along the woven threads, both lengthwise and crosswise. Bias is diagonal to the straight grains (true bias forms a 45° angle to both the crosswise and the lengthwise grains).

Place a square or rectangular template so that all edges are on the straight grain (Fig. 1, a).

With a triangle, you have a choice. You can place the template so that the longest edge is on the straight grain (b), or you can have the two short edges on the straight grain (c). Try to be consistent in placing triangles.

With a diamond, you also have two choices. You can place two edges on the straight grain (d), or you can have the straight grain running through the center of the diamond (e). Try to be consistent in placing diamonds.

Leave space around each template so you can add a seam allowance of ¼" to ½" when cutting the fabric.

Trace templates

Trace around each template. Use a No. 2 pencil on light fabrics and a colored pencil on dark fabrics—and keep those pencils sharpened. When all else fails, use a sliver of soap.

Try slipping a sheet of fine sandpaper, face up, under the fabric to keep the fabric from shifting.

Cut fabric

When you cut the fabric, use your eye to add a seam allowance of ¼" to ½". (After stitching, the seam allowance will be trimmed to ¼" or a little less, so it's not necessary to measure it exactly for cutting.)

Experienced quilters cut ¼" seam allowances. In my beginner classes, however, I find that people feel more secure with ½" seam allowances for pieced work. There is more fabric to hang onto when pinning and stitching, and there's also room for error. If someone accidentally cuts on the pencil line (and someone always does), she can shift the template, retrace and cut again; she still has fabric left for a ¼" seam allowance.

Pin-baste

After you have cut out all the pieces, lay them in front of you, face up, to form the block design. Pick up two adjoining pieces and position them with right sides together, ready for pinning. Place pin 1 on the pencil point (end of seam) at the right corner (Fig. 2). Check the other side to make sure the pin is going exactly into the pencil point on that piece also. Now bring the pin out horizontally along the pencil line. Position pin 2 vertically to anchor pin 1.

Put pin 3 on the pencil point at the opposite end of the seam, making sure the pin goes through the pencil point on the other side. Bring this pin out vertically.

Go back and place pins 4 and 5 horizontally to hold the pencil lines together. Add any more pins you may need along this seam line.

After you have pinned and stitched a number of pieces, there will be seams to match and pin-baste. Take special care with these. Place a pin through both seam lines (Fig. 3, a), then bring it back through the stitching on both layers (Fig. 3, b). You can avoid a pile-up of fabric by turning the seam allowances in opposite directions.

Stitch seams

For piecing, either by machine or by hand, I like to use regular white thread throughout so I don't have to change thread. If many of the quilt fabrics are dark, I may choose a medium color thread

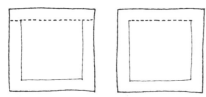

a. by machine   b. by hand

Fig. 4   *Stitching seams*

Fig. 5   *Running stitch*

Fig. 6   *Backstitch*

that blends better with most of the fabrics.

For most machine stitching, start at the raw edge. Set the machine for a small stitch (about 10 stitches to the inch) and sew along the pencil line. Stitch over vertical pins. When you come to a horizontal pin, stop the machine, keep the needle in the fabric and remove the pin. Continue stitching to the raw edge (Fig. 4, a).

For hand stitching, sew only from pencil point to pencil point; do not stitch into the seam allowances (Fig. 4, b). Use a small, even running stitch (Fig. 5), beginning and ending with small backstitches (Fig. 6) to secure the seam.

Trim seams and press

As soon as you stitch each seam, trim the seam allowances to ¼″ or a little less, and finger-press both edges to one side (preferably the darker side).

If you happen to be one of those rare people who has a love affair with an iron, you can press each seam to one side as you finish stitching. Not being one of those people, I content myself with finger-pressing until I am ready to put all my blocks or quilt sections together. Then I press everything with an iron to get out all the wrinkles. And I do mean *press*—lift the iron and set it down gently; don't iron back and forth.

Form rows or units

In piecing blocks, try to join small shapes to form rows or larger units. Then stitch the rows or units together to complete the block.

Piecing diamonds

When you piece diamonds to form such things as stars or flowers, you have many seams meeting at a center point (Figs. 7 and 8). To keep these points sharp, and to enable you to piece in squares and triangles

Fig. 7   *Star formed with diamonds*

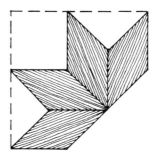

Fig. 8   *Flower formed with diamonds*

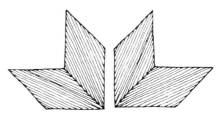

Fig. 9   *Joining pairs of diamonds*

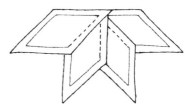

Fig. 10   *Pressing all seams in same direction*

Fig. 11 *Adding squares and triangles to star*

Fig. 12 *Adding a square and triangles to flower*

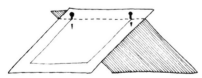

Fig. 13 *Stitching diamonds to form rows*

Fig. 14 *Joining rows of small diamonds*

between the diamonds, stitch only on the seam lines—never into the seam allowances. (Hand stitching is always done this way, but for diamonds, even machine stitching must begin and end exactly on pencil points.)

Begin a flower or star

Follow steps for *General piecing* through *Pin-baste*.

Working with pairs of diamonds (Fig. 9), stitch them together from point to point; do not stitch into seam allowances. Backstitch to secure, and trim the seam allowances to $1/8''$.

Repeat the step with the next pair of diamonds. Then join the two pairs to make a flower or half a star. Press all seams in one direction (Fig. 10).

If you are not making a star, skip the next section and continue with *Add triangles and squares*.

Complete a star

Join two more pairs of diamonds to complete another half star. To join the two halves, pin the seam lines together, matching pencil points.

I like to sew this seam by hand, even though I do the rest of the piecing by machine. For hand stitching, begin at one end (on the pencil point) and sew to the center. Slide the needle under the intersecting seam allowances (keep them free) and continue sewing to the end of the seam. Backstitch to secure.

If you want to use the machine, stitch from one seam end to the center, then turn the unit over and stitch from the opposite seam end to the center. Backstitch at the beginning and end of each stitching line.

Trim seam allowances to $1/8''$ and finger-press, keeping all seam allowances turned in the same direction.

To flatten the star center, place your thumb on the center and turn it, pressing in the direction of the seam allowances. There, no lumps in the center of your star!

Add triangles and squares

These pieces are added in two steps. First, pin one side of a square or triangle to one side of each diamond, right sides together (Figs. 11 and 12). Stitch on the pencil lines, going from the outside tip of the diamond to the point where two diamonds meet; do not stitch into seam allowances. Backstitch and stop.

Then pin and stitch the next side of the square or triangle to the adjoining diamond in the same way. The square or triangle should fit perfectly.

Rows of diamonds

Sometimes a large diamond is divided into small diamonds. In this case, the first step in piecing is to stitch the small diamonds together.

First join the diamonds to form rows. Pin-baste small diamonds with right sides together, matching pencil lines and end points. If you machine-stitch these seams, stitch from raw edge to raw edge, as in Fig. 13. (Yes, stitch into the seam allowances.) Complete one row, trim seam allowances to $1/8''$ and finger-press all the seams in one direction.

Complete remaining rows (Fig. 14). When you finger-press seam allowances, try to alternate seam direction in adjoining rows, pressing one row up and the next row down. This avoids bunching of fabric.

When all rows are completed, stitch them together, carefully matching adjoining seam lines. If you stitch by machine, begin and end each seam at the raw edges. Trim seams to $1/8''$ and finger-press to one side.

Once the large diamond is together, follow directions for piecing stars or flowers as outlined above.

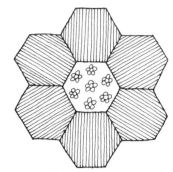

Fig. 15 *Piecing hexagons*

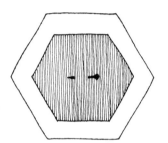

Fig. 16 *Using paper template to cut fabric*

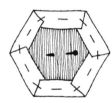

Fig. 17 *Basting fabric over template*

Fig. 18 *Whipping stitch*

English piecing

Many-sided pieces such as hexagons (Fig. 15) are difficult to piece by the usual method because they lose their exact shape in handling. To make it easier, we do English piecing.

For this, you baste each fabric piece to a paper template, which is left in place until all the pieces are joined.

Multiple templates

Instead of tracing the poster board or plastic template on fabric, use it on typing-weight paper—and trace a paper template for every piece of fabric needed. Cut out the papers accurately.

Cut and prepare fabric

Pin paper templates to the wrong side of the fabric. Cut out each shape, adding at least ¼″ seam allowance (Fig. 16).

Fold the seam allowance over the paper and baste—right through the paper (Fig. 17). Be sure that each corner is secure.

Following the quilt block design, work with two adjacent pieces and pin the right sides together. Use matching thread and join the edges with small whipping stitches (Fig. 18). Sew only into the folds. Try not to catch the paper (but if you do, it's no crime).

After the design has been built up, press the work with the papers still inside. Then snip and remove the basting threads, and the papers will pop right out. Everybody loves doing this paperwork—and you will, too.

Appliqué

Appliqué means sewing one piece of fabric, usually a free-form shape such as a flower, to another piece of fabric. I've divided this work into three types—Simple Appliqués, Intricate Shapes and Picture Appliqués.

If you're working on Intricate Shapes or Picture Appliqués, your first step will be to make a template of the whole shape or the whole picture for marking placement lines on the background fabric. (See *Position appliqué pieces*, page 7.) Then you'll be ready to proceed as follows.

Position templates

Place each template, face up, on the right side of the fabric, leaving enough room to add a ¼″ seam allowance when cutting the fabric. If possible, line up the center of the template with the straight grain of the fabric (Fig. 19).

Trace templates

Trace around each template, using a No. 2 pencil on light fabrics and a colored pencil on dark fabrics.

Cut and prepare appliqué

Cut out each appliqué, using your eye to add a ¼″ seam allowance.

To make turning easier, you can stay-stitch—an optional step. By machine or with very small hand stitches, go around the appliqué just outside the pencil line (Fig. 20).

Next, turn the seam allowance to the wrong side along the pencil line (any stay-stitching will be turned under), crease the edge and baste. I usually crease the fabric with my fingernail as I work, creasing a little, then basting a little.

When an appliqué has a V point or an inside curve, you must slash the seam allowance almost to the seam line so that the fabric can spread as you turn it (Figs. 20 and 21). Be

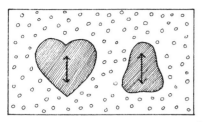

Fig. 19 *Positioning appliqué templates*

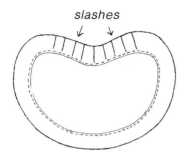

slashes

Fig. 20 *Stay-stitching and slashing seam allowances*

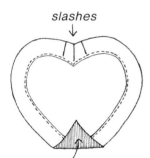

slashes

Fig. 21 *Turning point to wrong side*

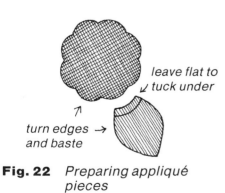

leave flat to tuck under

turn edges and baste

Fig. 22 *Preparing appliqué pieces*

careful not to slash through the seam line.

When the appliqué has a point, first turn the seam allowance at the point (Fig. 21). Then turn the seam allowance on either side of the point to enclose the raw edges.

Sometimes part of one appliqué will be covered by another, as when a leaf is partially covered by a flower. In that case, do not turn all edges of the lower appliqué. Leave flat any underlap (the portion that will be covered), as in Fig. 22.

After basting appliqué pieces, press each shape with an iron.

Making perfect circles

This method works for circles, but you also can use it for other rounded shapes such as leaves.

Make the template for circle or leaf from a file folder or an index card (paper is too thin and poster board is too thick). Pin the template (face down if leaf is not symmetrical) to the wrong side of the fabric. Cut out, allowing at least 1″ seam allowance all around.

By hand or machine, sew gathering stitches around the shape, about ¼″ beyond the template (Fig. 23). Pull threads to gather fabric firmly around the template (Fig. 24). With an iron, press the edge on both sides.

Remove the pin and pull out the template. Press the fabric again and trim the seam allowance to ¼″. (Part of your stitching line may be cut away, but that's all right.) And there you have it—a perfect circle or leaf.

Position appliqué pieces

Simple Appliqués like the Rose Wreath (Fig. 25) can be placed on the background square "by eye." To make placement easy, fold the background square in half, matching pencil seam lines. Put a pin through matching corners, exactly on the corner points, and finger-press the fold. Next, fold the square into

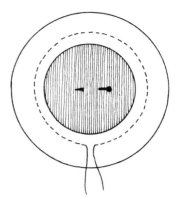

Fig. 23 *Sewing a gathering line around template*

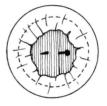

Fig. 24 *Gathering fabric over template*

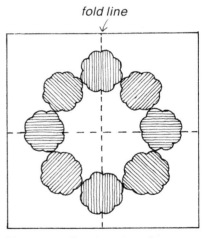

fold line

Fig. 25 *Positioning Simple Appliqués*

Fig. 26 *Cutting out whole Intricate Shape*

Fig. 27 *Cutting large shape apart to get separate templates*

Fig. 28 *Making full-drawing template for Picture Appliqué*

quarters, lining up corner points and seam lines, and finger-press the folds. Open the square.

To make diagonal guidelines, fold the square on the diagonal, matching pencil lines and corner points, and finger-press the fold. Repeat to mark the other diagonal line.

Use these folds as guides for positioning and pinning appliqué pieces in place.

Intricate Shapes like Lady Jane (Fig. 26) will have one large shape that's divided into various overlapping pieces. Your first step is to make a template of the whole shape, being sure to copy all inside lines. Center this whole shape on the background fabric. Trace around it lightly, using a No. 5H or 6H pencil (or a silver pencil on dark fabric). Then carefully cut the large template apart, making a separate template for each fabric piece (Fig. 27).

Now you're ready to cut and prepare appliqué pieces. (See preceding directions.) When positioning appliqués on the background square, keep them within the lines you have drawn and pin in place.

Picture Appliqués like Birds in the Tree (Fig. 28) will have some pieces overlapping and other pieces connected by embroidery stitches.

Your first step is to make a complete drawing of the picture, and this is the method I like best. On a 15″ square of tracing paper (or shelf paper you can see through), trace the complete pattern.

Next, make a full-picture template by transferring the tracing to a 15″square of poster board, using regular carbon paper under your tracing. Remove the tracing and carbon, and go over the lines with a pen to make them stand out.

Place the whole template, face down, on the wrong side of the background fabric, keeping edges on the straight grain. Tape template to fabric, and trace around edges with a pen-

cil to mark seam lines. With template still in place, cut out fabric, adding ¼″ to ½″ seam allowances.

Turn fabric over so you can see the design through the fabric. Very lightly, copy the whole design with a sharp No. 5H or 6H pencil. Remove fabric.

Finally, cut the large template apart to make a template for each shape.

Now you're ready to cut and prepare appliqué pieces. (See preceding directions.) As you position appliqués on the background square, keep them within the lines you have drawn and pin in place.

Note: All Picture Appliqués shown in the book are done on off-white background squares. If you use a dark background fabric (one that you can't see through), you will need another method for drawing guidelines. You can position your paper tracing directly on the right side of the fabric, slip dressmaker's carbon between the layers and go over the pattern lines with a dry ball-point pen.

You will still need to make individual templates for each fabric piece needed.

Attach appliqués

For the *appliqué stitch* (Fig. 29), choose regular sewing thread in a color that matches the appliqué fabric. Thread a quilting needle with a single strand and knot one end.

Begin the stitch by bringing the needle up through the background fabric, into the folded edge of the appliqué. Put the needle back into the background fabric, just below where thread came out. Take a slanting stitch, coming up through the folded edge of the appliqué, about ⅛″ ahead. Keep your stitches small, and they will "melt" into the fabric.

Look at the back of your work and you'll see the slanting stitches; the stitches on the right side should be almost invisible.

Directions for appliqué projects in this book follow the

Fig. 29 *Appliqué stitch*

Fig. 30 *Buttonhole stitch*

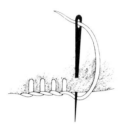

Fig. 31 *Blanket stitch*

Fig. 32 *Chain stitch*

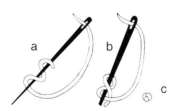

Fig. 33 *French knot*

Fig. 34 *Satin stitch*

usual method of adding seam allowances and attaching pieces with the appliqué stitch. However, there may be times when you want to vary this method.

Sometimes, when I'm making a quilt or wall hanging that will be dry-cleaned (not washed), I may work with raw edges. I cut an appliqué shape right on the pencil line and attach it with a close *buttonhole stitch* (Fig. 30). This method is handy when appliqués have many little points, such as holly leaves, that are difficult to turn. If you do leave the edges raw, you must have very firm fabric and you must keep your buttonhole stitches very close together.

To make a buttonhole stitch, thread an embroidery needle with two strands of embroidery floss and knot one end. Bring the needle up through the background fabric, just below the raw edge of the appliqué. Working from left to right, hold the thread down with your left thumb (if you're right-handed). Insert the needle in the appliqué, about ¼″ above where the thread came out, making a vertical stitch. Bring the needle out under the raw edge and over the thread, into the loop that is formed. Continue making stitches, keeping them even and very close together.

Sometimes you may want to use an embroidery stitch for attaching an appliqué, even though you have turned under the seam allowance. In that case, you can use the *blanket stitch* (Fig. 3l). This is worked the same as a buttonhole stitch, but the stitches are not so close together—they can be ⅛″ apart.

More embroidery stitches

To embroider design lines on an appliqué, I often use the *chain stitch* (Fig. 32). Thread an embroidery needle with two strands of embroidery thread and knot one end. Begin by bringing the needle up through the background fabric at the

top of the design line. Hold the thread down with your thumb. Put the needle back in, right beside where it came out, and take another stitch, bringing the needle over the thread to form a loop. Continue in the same way, taking each stitch inside the previous loop to form a chain.

To embroider the center of flowers, you can make *French knots* (Fig. 33). Thread an embroidery needle with two strands of floss and knot one end. Bring the needle up through the fabric. Wrap the thread twice around the needle, close to the fabric (a), then insert the needle in the fabric, almost where the thread came out (b). Pull the thread to the back, forming a decorative knot on the surface (c).

To fill in areas, such as a bird's beak, work the *satin stitch* (Fig. 34). Use two strands of embroidery floss and knot one end. Bring the needle up through the fabric at one side of the design. Take a long stitch across the design, inserting the needle and carrying the thread under the work. Bring the needle up again, just below the previous stitch. Keep stitches close together to fill in the design.

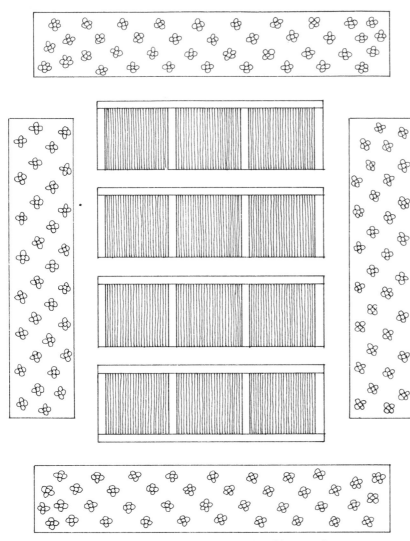

Fig. 35 *Some large quilts can be quilted in sections, then stitched together.*

Some final notes

The sampler quilts in the next section have blocks that require several levels of skill, and I've tried to arrange the blocks for each quilt from the easiest to the most challenging. If you decide that you don't want to make a certain block—maybe it doesn't appeal to you, or it looks too difficult—don't worry. Just pick a substitute. You can repeat a block from the same quilt, or borrow a block from one of the other samplers. All blocks in the sampler quilts are 15″ square, so they can be interchanged to suit you.

The large quilts in this book fit most standard double beds, hanging almost to the floor, and they fit queen-size beds when used with a dust ruffle. It's always best to measure your bed before you begin. You can make any needed adjustments to the size of your quilt by adding to or subtracting from the borders.

This chapter has described the basic techniques you'll need for making the quilt tops (including wall hangings) in the next section. Directions for quilting and finishing the projects are given in Chapter 12, page 147.

For some large quilts, you will have a choice of two quilting methods. You can assemble the whole top and then quilt it, or you can quilt smaller sections (Fig. 35) and then stitch the sections together. Both methods are covered in Chapter 12.

Now, which quilt or wall hanging are you going to make first?

Hummingbird, page 16

Winged Square, page 16

Bird's Nest, page 17

Birds on the Ground, page 17

American Eagle, page 18

Wild Goose Chase (block), page 18

11

Geese, page 19

Dove of Peace, page 19

Dove in the Window, page 20

Owl, page 20

Rooster, page 21

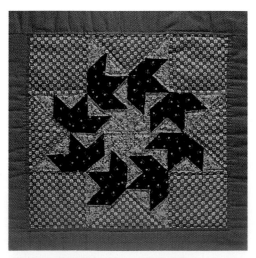

Flying Swallows, page 22

FOR THE BIRDS SAMPLER QUILT _____

Goose Tracks, page 22

Partridge in a Pear Tree, page 23

Birds in the Tree, page 23

Birds in Air, page 24

CHRISTMAS SAMPLER QUILT _____

Night and Noon, page 46

Rose Wreath, page 46

2 For the Birds Sampler Quilt

Like many other quilters who enjoy using traditional patterns, I decided to make a Wild Goose Chase quilt with vertical rows of "geese." It seemed like a wonderful way to use some of my scraps, so I started piecing triangles to make rectangles (see Fig. 31).

After doing this for a while, it dawned on me just how many rectangles I would have to piece. I thought, "This is for the birds."

I decided to use the Wild Goose Chase rows for a border on a sampler quilt of bird blocks. The final quilt has 12 center blocks and four corner blocks. One section of the border, of course, is the pieced Wild Goose Chase. For colors, I chose peach, dark blue and soft green.

I like to combine many fabrics in a quilt, and this one is no exception. There are 20 different fabrics, mostly prints, plus off-white, and all of these are used in the Wild Goose Chase border. You may want to use fewer fabrics, and that's all right. Just repeat them more often in the various blocks.

You can sew the whole top together before quilting, or you can quilt in sections. You may want to read about the two methods in Chapter 12 before you begin.

The finished quilt is 87x105".

Materials
(Yardage is for fabric 45" wide.)

2½ yd. dark fabric with narrow stripes, for borders
3 yd. solid color or fabric with small dots, for sashing and bias binding
2 yd. off-white solid, for background squares and some piecing
¼ yd. each of 10 medium-to-dark fabrics (prints, solids)*
¼ yd. each of 8 lighter fabrics (prints, solids)*
7½ yd. print or solid, for backing, if you plan to assemble the whole top before quilting (*or* 10 yd. if you plan to quilt in sections)
Thread for piecing in white or blending color
Thread for appliqué in matching colors
Quilting thread in white or colors
Embroidery floss in black, plus cream, rust and green (or colors to match your own fabrics)
Polyester batting: 1 pkg. 90x108", if you plan to assemble the whole top before quilting (*or* 1 pkg. 90x108" and ½ pkg. 72x90", if you plan to quilt in sections)

* *This is a general guide for yardage. You may wish to use more than ¼ yd. of some fabrics.*

Prepare fabric

Prewash all the fabric if you plan to wash the finished quilt. Then cut off sections which will be used later for making sashing, borders and appliqué blocks.

From striped border fabric, cut 2¼ yd. for borders.

From sashing fabric, cut 1¾ yd. for sashing and a 34" square for bias.

From off-white solid, cut a section 32x48" to use as background fabric for appliqué blocks.

Set aside these sections and use remaining lengths for making the blocks and border strips that follow.

Make blocks and piece border

Directions suggest the number of light, medium and dark colors needed for each block. You can use prints or solids, or a mix. When there is more than one fabric in a color group, it helps to number them—light color #1, light color #2, etc.

For tips on making templates, piecing blocks and doing appliqué, see Chapter 1.

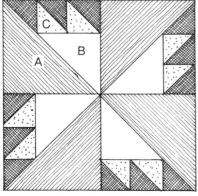

Fig. 1 *HUMMINGBIRD*
(color photo, page 11)

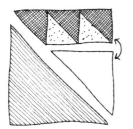

Fig. 2 *Piecing corner square*

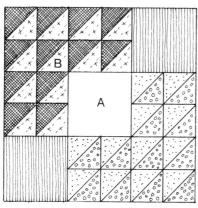

Fig. 3 *WINGED SQUARE*
(color photo, page 11)

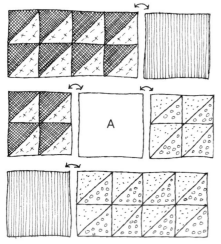

Fig. 4 *Piecing block*

HUMMINGBIRD

The first design is a simple pieced block with 28 triangles, all cut from three patterns. Choose four fabrics—one light color, two medium and one dark.

Make templates

Trace patterns A-C, page 27, and make templates.

Cut fabric

Place templates on the wrong side of the fabric and trace. Cut out, adding ¼″ to ½″ seam allowances:

    4 A triangles of medium color #1
    4 B triangles of light color
    8 C triangles of medium color # 2
    12 C triangles of dark color

Assemble

Lay all pieces, face up, to form the block in Fig. 1. Work on one corner section at a time (Fig. 2).

First pin-baste and stitch each medium color C triangle to a dark C triangle to make two squares. Trim each seam and finger-press to the dark side. Then join the squares and add the end triangle to make a row.

Join the completed row to a B triangle to form a larger triangle. Then add an A triangle to form a square.

Complete all four corner squares. Check the position of the squares and stitch them together to form two horizontal rows. Join the two rows and you have the Hummingbird.

WINGED SQUARE

Two patterns, a square and a triangle, are all you need for piecing Winged Square. Choose six fabrics—one light color, four medium and one dark.

Make templates

Trace patterns A and B, page 28, and make templates.

Cut fabric

Place templates on the wrong side of the fabric and trace. Cut out, adding ¼″ to ½″ seam allowances:

    1 A square of light color
    2 A squares of medium color #1
    12 B triangles of medium color #2
    12 B triangles of medium color #3
    12 B triangles of medium color #4
    12 B triangles of dark color

Assemble

First stitch all those triangles together to form squares. Pin-baste each dark color B to a medium color #2 B. If you use a machine, feed the triangles, a pair at a time, under the presser foot to stitch the diagonal seams. Don't cut the thread until you're done. Then snip the pairs apart, trim the seams and finger-press to the darker side.

Repeat the step to join remaining pairs of B triangles.

Now lay all the pieces, face up, to form the block, following Fig. 4 as a guide. Note that the dark triangles are grouped in the upper left corner. Keep each fabric in the same position throughout.

Stitch the small squares together to form rows, then join the rows to form units. Stitch units to the A pieces to form three horizontal rows. Finally, join the three rows to complete the block.

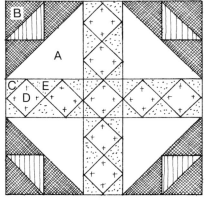

Fig. 5 ***BIRD'S NEST***
(color photo, page 11)

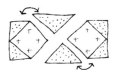

Fig. 6 *Piecing corner*

Fig. 7 *Piecing rectangle*

Fig. 8 *Piecing center*

Fig. 9 ***BIRDS ON THE GROUND***
(color photo, page 11)

BIRD'S NEST

Here's another block pieced from squares and triangles. To make it, choose five fabrics—three light colors, one medium and one dark.

Make templates

Trace patterns A-E, page 29, and make templates.

Cut fabric

Place templates on the wrong side of the fabric and trace. Cut out, adding ¼" to ½" seam allowances:

4 A triangles of light color #1
12 B triangles of dark color
4 B triangles of light color #2
20 C triangles of medium color
9 D squares of light color #3
8 E triangles of medium color

Assemble

Lay all pieces, face up, to form the design in Fig. 5. Begin with a corner. Join three dark B triangles to one light color B triangle (Fig. 6). Stitch this to an A triangle to form a corner square. Repeat to complete three more corner squares.

Next, work with a rectangle (Fig. 7). First stitch two C triangles to each square. Add an E triangle to each D, then join the two units to make the rectangle. Repeat to complete three more rectangles.

Piece the center by stitching four C triangles to the D square (Fig. 8).

Form top and bottom rows of the block by stitching corner squares to a rectangle (see Fig. 5). Form a center row by stitching the two remaining rectangles to the center square. Finally, join the horizontal rows to complete the Bird's Nest block.

BIRDS ON THE GROUND

Ten little birds are cut from a single pattern and placed at random on this corner appliqué block. Reverse the pattern for four birds, so they'll face in the opposite direction.

Choose 10 appliqué fabrics, mixing light, medium and dark colors, and sew them to an off-white background.

Make template

Trace pattern, page 28, and make a template. Also draft a 15" square on poster board or plastic and cut out. Use this for marking the background fabric, and save it for use later.

Cut fabric

Place the 15"-square template on the wrong side of the off-white solid fabric and trace. Cut out, adding ¼" to ½" seam allowances.

Place the bird template on the right side of the appliqué fabrics and trace. Cut out, adding ¼" seam allowances:

6 birds
4 birds (reversed)

Assemble

Stay-stitch appliqués (optional) and slash seam allowances into V points and inside curves. Turn seam allowances, baste and press.

Position bird appliqués on background fabric, keeping them at least ½" from seam lines. Move birds around to balance the colors and vary the slant of their bodies (Fig. 9).

Sew pieces to background, using matching thread and the appliqué stitch (page 8).

To outline each wing, mark the line by eye, or make a template and trace it with a pencil. Embroider with contrasting floss (I used rust) and a chain stitch (page 9).

Lightly draw lines for legs, feet and beaks. To embroider, use the same floss and single straight stitches. On a few birds, I drew closed beaks and

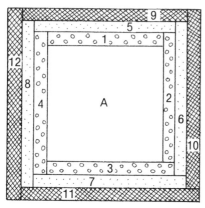

Fig. 10 AMERICAN EAGLE
(color photo, page 11)

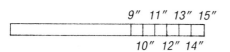

Fig. 11 *Making ruler template*

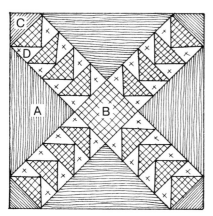

Fig. 12 WILD GOOSE CHASE (block)
(color photo, page 11)

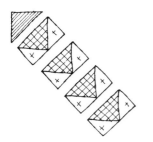

Fig. 13 *Piecing strip*

embroidered them with satin stitches (page 9). See pattern for Birds in the Tree, page 66, as a guide. For eyes, use floss and French knots (page 9).

For a final touch, use a pencil to draw one or two worms (see pattern on page 28). Embroider with green floss and about four chain stitches.

AMERICAN EAGLE

The magnificent eagle is a symbol of our country, and it has long been used as a quilting design. This one is quilted on an off-white center square, and it has a triple frame of three fabrics—one light color, one medium and one dark.

Make templates

Patterns for the center square and long framing strips are easy to draft. For the center A template, draw a 9" square on poster board or plastic and cut out.

The framing strips are 1" wide, cut in seven different lengths. Instead of drafting seven templates, you can draw one to use for all lengths. On poster board or plastic, measure a rectangle 1" wide and 15" long (Fig. 11). On the strip, measure up 9" and mark a line across the template. Add additional marks for 10", 11", 12", 13" and 14". Measure accurately. You are really making a ruler.

Cut fabric

Place templates on the wrong side of the fabric and trace. Use ruler template to mark needed strips. Cut out, adding ¼" to ½" seam allowances:
  1 A square of off-white solid
  1 strip, 1x9", of medium color
  2 strips, 1x10" each, of medium color
  1 strip, 1x11", of medium color

1 strip, 1x11", of light color
2 strips, 1x12" each, of light color
1 strip, 1x13", of light color
1 strip, 1x13", of dark color
2 strips, 1x14" each, of dark color
1 strip, 1x15", of dark color

Assemble

Lay all pieces, face up, to form the block in Fig. 10. Medium color strips form the inside frame, light color strips are next and dark strips are on the outside.

Stitch first strip to top of center square. Continue adding strips, working clockwise and following numbers on the diagram.

The eagle design will be marked and quilted later.

WILD GOOSE CHASE (block)

Sometimes traditional patterns were used in a variety of ways, and this is a good example. Instead of piecing the geese triangles to fly in straight rows, they are arranged to crisscross for a block design.

Choose three fabrics—one light color, one medium and one dark.

Make templates

Trace patterns A-D, page 31, and make templates.

Cut fabric

Place templates on the wrong side of the fabric and trace. Cut out, adding ¼" to ½" seam allowances:
  4 A triangles of dark color
  1 B square of medium color
  4 C triangles of dark color
  16 C triangles of medium color
  32 D triangles of light color

Assemble

Lay all pieces, face up, to form the block in Fig. 12. Work with each group of four medium color C triangles and eight D triangles (Fig. 13).

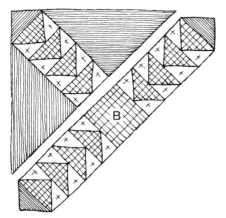

Fig. 14 *Forming diagonal rows*

Fig. 15 ***GEESE***
(color photo, page 12)

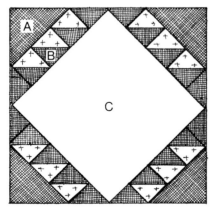

Fig. 16 ***DOVE OF PEACE***
(color photo, page 12)

Stitch the triangles together to form rectangles, then join the rectangles. Add a dark C to the end of each strip (this is a corner of the block).

In the upper left corner, add an A triangle to each side of the strip to form a large triangle (Fig. 14). Repeat to make a second large triangle in the lower right corner.

Stitch the two remaining strips to the center B square (Fig 14). Now sew the three diagonal rows together to complete the block.

GEESE

A pair of wild geese waddle across one corner of the quilt. Choose three fabrics for the appliqués—a medium and a dark color for the birds, and another medium color for the beaks and feet.

Make template

Before you begin, read directions for *Intricate Shapes*, page 8. Trace pattern for geese, pages 32-33, joining the sections on broken lines. Make one template of the whole design.

You'll also need your 15"-square template for the background.

Cut fabric

Place the 15" square on the wrong side of the off-white fabric and trace. Cut out, adding ¼" to ½" seam allowances.

Turn the background fabric right side up. Center the geese template on top and trace around it lightly. Then cut the template apart to get individual templates.

Place each shape, face up, on the right side of the fabric and trace. Cut out, adding ¼" seam allowances:

    1 goose A of dark color
    1 goose B of medium
       color #1
    4 feet of medium color #2
    2 beaks of medium color #2

Assemble

Stay-stitch appliqué pieces (optional) and slash seam allowances into V points and inside curves. Turn seam allowances (unless they tuck under other pieces), baste and press.

Position appliqué pieces on the off-white square, using your pencil lines as a guide. Pin in place.

Sew appliqués to background fabric, beginning with the bottom layers. Use matching thread and the appliqué stitch (page 8).

To mark wing design on goose A, carefully cut the body template apart along the design. Position template on top of the appliqué and trace the line with a colored pencil. Embroider with contrasting floss (I used cream) and the chain stitch (page 9). Embroider the eyes with floss and the satin stitch (page 9).

DOVE OF PEACE

Here's another block with a bird quilted on the off-white center square. The dove is surrounded by triangles cut from two fabrics—one light color and one dark.

Make templates

Trace patterns A and B, page 35, and make templates. Also draft a 10⅝" C square on poster board or plastic, and cut out.

Cut fabric

Place templates on the wrong side of the fabric and trace. Cut out, adding ¼" to ½" seam allowances:

    4 A triangles of dark color
    20 B triangles of dark color
    12 B triangles of light color
    1 C square of off-white

Assemble

Lay pieces, face up, to form the block in Fig. 16. Look carefully at the diagram. At

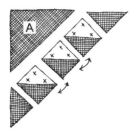

Fig. 17 *Piecing corner*

Fig. 18 **DOVE IN THE WINDOW**
(color photo, page 12)

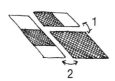

Fig. 19 *Adding rows to large diamond*

first, you may think all the corners are the same, but they're not. There are two different arrangements of triangles—opposite corners are the same.

Work on one corner at a time (Fig. 17). Stitch small B triangles together to make squares. Then stitch the squares together, and add the end triangles to form a row. Add an A triangle to make a large corner triangle.

Finally, stitch corner triangles to the center square, with dark triangles next to the off-white square.

The dove will be traced and quilted later.

DOVE IN THE WINDOW

The basic shape of this block is an eight-pointed star, with each star point made up of one large diamond and five small ones. The four doves are formed by using colors for some of the diamonds.

You'll need four different fabrics. Use a light print for the large squares and triangles, off-white for some diamonds, and a medium color and a dark color for the doves.

Make templates
Trace patterns A-D, page 35, and make templates. (Note that the A square and B triangle are also used for another block called Flying Swallows.)

Cut fabric
Place templates on the wrong side of the fabric and trace. Cut out, adding ¼″ to ½″ seam allowances:

    4 A squares of light print
    4 B triangles of light print
    2 C diamonds of dark color
    2 C diamonds of medium color
    4 C diamonds of off-white solid
    8 D diamonds of dark color
    8 D diamonds of medium color
    24 D diamonds of off-white solid

Assemble
Lay all pieces, face up, to form the block in Fig. 18. Notice that the body and tail of each dove are in the same star point, but the wings are in adjacent star points. Watch color placement, and be sure the dark birds have dark wings.

Work on one star point at a time. First join small diamonds to form two rows (Fig. 19), matching pencil lines and end points. If you use a machine, stitch from raw edge to raw edge.

Stitch the rows to the C diamond in the same way.

Join the large star points, being careful not to stitch into the seam allowances. (See *Piecing diamonds,* page 4.)

Finally, piece in the large squares and triangles. Now, isn't that an interesting block?

OWL

A wise old bird guards the upper left corner of the quilt. Scallops on his body are embroidered in the chain stitch.

Use five appliqué fabrics for the main pieces of the owl and tree branch—two medium colors and three dark. Add black and white for the eyes.

Make template
Before you begin, read directions for *Picture Appliqués,* page 8. Then trace pattern, pages 36-37, joining sections on broken lines. Transfer the tracing to a 15″ square of poster board. This will be your whole template.

Cut fabric
Place the whole template, face down, on the wrong side of the off-white solid. Tape template to fabric, and trace around the outside edges to mark seam lines. With the template still in place, cut out the fabric, adding ¼″ to ½″ seam allowances.

Turn poster board over, and you'll see the design through

Fig. 20 **OWL**
(color photo, page 12)

Fig. 21 **ROOSTER**
(color photo, page 12)

the fabric. With a sharp No. 5H or 6H pencil, lightly trace all the lines.

Now you can cut the large template apart to make individual templates. *Note:* First trace the whole face template, then cut the eyes and beak to layer on top.

Place templates, face up, on the right side of the fabric and trace. Cut out, adding ¼″ seam allowances:

    1 head of dark color #1
    1 face of dark color #1
    2 wings of dark color #2
    1 branch of dark color #3
    1 body of medium color #1
    2 feet of medium color #2
    1 beak of medium color #2
    2 outer eyes of white solid
    2 inner eyes of black solid

Assemble

Stay-stitch appliqué pieces (optional) and slash seam allowances into V points and inside curves. Turn seam allowances (unless they tuck under other pieces), baste and press. Leave both ends of branch flat. These will be caught in the seam allowances when block is stitched to sashing.

Position appliqué pieces on the off-white square, using your pencil lines as a guide. Pin in place.

Sew appliqués to background fabric, beginning with the bottom layers. Use matching thread and the appliqué stitch (page 8). For contrast, you may want to attach some pieces with floss and the blanket stitch (page 9).

To mark scallops on the body, carefully cut the body template apart on the design lines. Position each piece on top of the appliqué and trace the scalloped edge with a pencil. Use the same technique to mark design lines on wings.

To embroider these lines, use contrasting floss (mine was green) and the chain stitch (page 9). Add the eye highlights with white or cream floss and a straight stitch.

ROOSTER

This fancy bird shows off his plumage with the help of seven different fabrics—one light color, three medium and three dark. He's appliquéd to an off-white background.

Make template

Before you begin, read directions for *Intricate Shapes,* page 8. Trace pattern, pages 38-40, joining the three sections on broken lines. Make one template of the whole design.

You'll also need your 15″-square template for marking the background fabric.

Cut fabric

Place the 15″ square on the wrong side of the off-white fabric and trace. Cut out, adding ¼″ to ½″ seam allowances.

Turn the background fabric right side up. Center the whole rooster template on top, and trace around it with a sharp No. 5H or 6H pencil. Then cut the template apart to get individual templates.

Place each shape, face up, on the right side of the fabric and trace. Cut out, adding ¼″ seam allowances:

    1 head of dark color #1
    1 comb of medium color #1
    1 upper tail of medium
       color #1
    1 lower tail of dark color #2
    2 feet of dark color #3
    1 body of medium color #2
    1 wattle of medium color #2
    1 tail trim A of medium
       color #3
    1 tail trim B of medium
       color #3
    1 beak of light color

Assemble

Stay-stitch appliqué pieces (optional) and slash seam allowances into V points and inside curves. Turn seam allowances (unless they tuck under other pieces), baste and press.

Position appliqué pieces on the off-white square, using

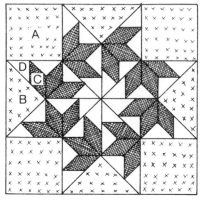

Fig. 22 FLYING SWALLOWS
(color photo, page 12)

Fig. 23 *Piecing large diamond*

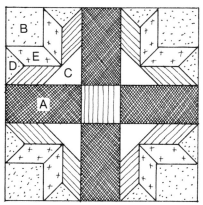

Fig. 24 GOOSE TRACKS
(color photo, page 13)

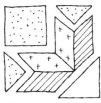

Fig. 25 *Piecing corner*

your pencil lines as a guide. Pin in place. (You can position the two tail trims A and B by eye.)

Sew appliqués to background fabric, beginning with the bottom layers. Use matching thread and the appliqué stitch (page 8), or floss with a blanket stitch (page 9).

To mark scallops on the body, carefully cut the body template apart on the design lines. Position each piece on top of the appliqué and trace the scalloped edge with a pencil. To embroider scallops, use cream color embroidery floss and a chain stitch (page 9). For eyes, use same floss and a satin stitch (page 9).

FLYING SWALLOWS

The large diamonds in this eight-pointed star are divided into small diamonds and triangles. Look closely, and you'll see the swallows. Each one is formed of three dark diamonds.

Choose three fabrics—one light color, one medium and one dark.

Make templates
Trace patterns A-D, page 35, and make templates. (Note that the A square and B triangle are also used for the Dove in the Window block.)

Cut fabric
Place templates on the wrong side of the fabric and trace. Cut out, adding ¼″ to ½″ seam allowances:

    4 A squares of medium color
    4 B triangles of medium color
    24 C diamonds of dark color
    32 D triangles of light color

Assemble
Lay pieces, face up, to form block in Fig. 22, and work with one large star point (Fig. 23). Join the three diamonds, being

sure not to stitch into seam allowances. (See *Piecing diamonds,* page 4.)

Piece in two small D triangles, keeping the long sides of the triangles on the outside. Add a D triangle to each end.

That completes one large diamond. All you need are seven more.

Finally, join the large diamonds, then add the large squares and triangles to complete the block. Your swallows are all flying.

GOOSE TRACKS

The E shapes in this design may look like diamonds, but they are really rhomboids (adjacent sides are of different lengths). For that reason, you must reverse the E template when tracing it on fabric. When you piece the block, however, handle those rhomboids just like diamonds.

Choose five fabrics—two light colors, two medium and one dark.

Make templates
Trace patterns A-E, page 41, and make templates.

Cut fabric
Place templates on wrong side of fabric and trace. Cut out, adding ¼″ to ½″ seam allowances:

    4 A rectangles of dark color
    1 B square of medium color #1
    4 B squares of medium color #2
    4 C triangles of light color #1
    8 D triangles of medium color #2
    4 E rhomboids of light color #2
    4 E (reversed) of light color #2
    4 E rhomboids of medium color #1
    4 E (reversed) of medium color #1

Fig. 26 *PARTRIDGE IN A PEAR TREE* (color photo, page 13)

Fig. 27 *BIRDS IN THE TREE* (color photo, page 13)

Assemble

Lay all pieces, face up, to form the block in Fig. 24, with the light color E rhomboids between medium E rhomboids.

Begin with one corner section (Fig. 25). Join the four E pieces, stitching only from end point to end point. (See *Piecing diamonds,* page 4.) Piece in two D triangles and a B square. Then add a C triangle.

You will need three more of these corner squares.

To form a top and bottom row, stitch a corner square to each long side of an A rectangle. For the middle row, stitch an A rectangle to each side of the B square. Then stitch the rows together.

PARTRIDGE IN A PEAR TREE

This design is good for all seasons. I used five appliqué fabrics—one light color, two medium (including rust for the pears and green for the leaves), and two dark. The background is off-white solid.

Make templates

Before you begin, read directions for *Picture Appliqués,* page 8. Then trace pattern, pages 42-43, joining sections on broken lines. Transfer tracing to a 15″ square of poster board to make a whole template.

Cut fabric

Place the whole template, face down, on the wrong side of the off-white solid. Tape template to fabric, and trace around the outside edges to mark seam lines. With template still in place, cut out the fabric, adding ¼″ to ½″ seam allowances.

Turn fabric over and you'll see the design through the fabric. Lightly trace all lines with a sharp No. 5H or 6H pencil.

Now you can cut the large template apart to make individual templates for the bird, tree and pears. There are three leaf patterns—A, B and C.

Place templates, face up, on the right side of the fabric and trace. Cut out, adding ¼″ seam allowances:

1 tree trunk of dark color #1
1 bird body of dark color #2
1 bird wing of light color
5 pears of medium color

To cut and form leaves, follow directions for *Making perfect circles,* page 7. You will need:

6 A leaves of green
5 B leaves of green
4 C leaves of green

Assemble

Stay-stitch appliqué pieces (optional) and slash into seam allowances at V points and inside curves. Turn seam allowances, baste and press.

Position appliqués on off-white square, using your pencil lines as a guide. Pin in place.

Sew pieces to background, using matching thread and the appliqué stitch (page 8). For contrast, you may want to attach some pieces with embroidery floss and the blanket stitch (page 9).

To embroider line for tree branch, use green floss and the chain stitch (page 9). For head and tail trims on bird, use floss (mine was rust) and the chain stitch. For beak, use the same floss and a satin stitch (page 9). For eye, use black floss and a French knot (page 9).

BIRDS IN THE TREE

This block also is used on the Christmas Sampler quilt. Follow the directions that begin on page 54, substituting fabric colors for this quilt.

Choose four appliqué fabrics, and cut the following pieces:

1 tree trunk of medium color #1
2 bird bodies of dark color
2 bird heads of medium color #2
2 bird wings of medium color #2
14 leaves of medium green

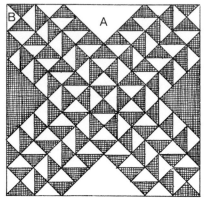

Fig. 28 *BIRDS IN AIR*
(color photo, page 13)

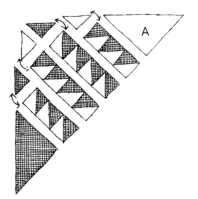

Fig. 29 *Piecing upper left corner*

Fig. 30 *Forming diagonal row*

Fig. 31 *WILD GOOSE CHASE (border)*

BIRDS IN AIR

When I first saw this block, I thought it was just little triangles sewn together willy-nilly. But when I started to draft the pattern, I was amazed at the cleverness of our great-grandmothers. The design is carefully planned.

There are 164 triangles, so this is a nice piecing challenge. Off-white triangles separate the colored triangles, and you can use as many different fabrics as you like.

I hope you've been saving all your little scraps—they'll come in handy now.

Make templates
Trace patterns A and B, page 41, and make templates.

Cut fabric
Place templates on the wrong side of the fabric and trace. Cut out, adding ¼″ to ½″ seam allowances:

  2 A triangles of off-white solid
  2 A triangles of one dark color
  80 B triangles of off-white solid
  80 B triangles of various colored fabrics (try to have a good mix of light, medium and dark)

Assemble
Set aside the large A triangles, plus 8 off-white and 8 colored B triangles.

Pin-baste and stitch each remaining colored triangle to an off-white triangle along the diagonal to make a square. If you use a machine, feed the triangles under the presser foot in pairs, and stitch a group of triangles before you cut the thread. After stitching, cut the pairs apart. Trim each seam and finger-press it to the darker side. You should have 72 little squares.

Lay all pieces, face up, to form the design in Fig. 28, arranging colors to suit you. Be sure the large A triangles are correctly placed.

Now let's work in sections, beginning with the upper left corner. First, join the squares to make rows, adding an extra triangle at the end of each row (Fig. 29). Stitch the rows together, keeping in mind that a colored triangle will always be against an off-white triangle. Then add the large A triangles, and you have a big corner triangle.

Repeat the steps to complete the lower right triangle.

Work on the remaining sections, first piecing the upper right corner (Fig. 30), and then the lower left corner. Finally, complete the center square. Stitch these three sections together to form a center diagonal row.

Add the big corner triangles to complete the block. Look at those birds fly!

WILD GOOSE CHASE (border)

Here's the pattern that inspired this whole quilt—a 3x6″ rectangle, divided into three triangles (Fig. 31). There are 88 of these rectangles in the quilt border—25 in each side section and 19 in both top and bottom sections.

I chose medium and dark colors for the A triangles and light colors for the B triangles, with a total of 11 different fabric combinations. All combinations were used eight times, repeated in the same sequence all around the quilt (see color photo, page 14).

You can use fewer fabric combinations, but try to have a number (such as 2, 4, 8 or 11) that will divide 88 evenly. For example, with four fabric combinations, each one would be used 22 times (88 divided by 4 equals 22).

    LET'S MAKE MORE PATCHWORK QUILTS

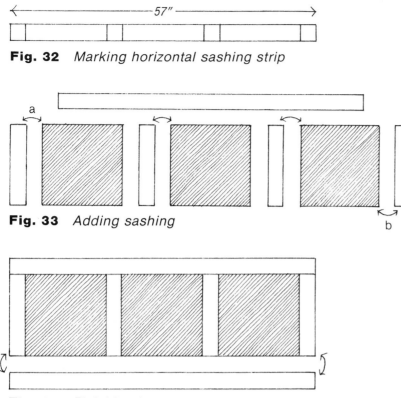

← ————57"———— →

Fig. 32 *Marking horizontal sashing strip*

Fig. 33 *Adding sashing*

Fig. 34 *Finishing bottom row*

Make templates
Trace patterns A and B, page 40, and make templates.

Cut fabric
Place templates on the wrong side of the fabric and trace. Cut out, adding ¼" to ½" seam allowances:

88 A triangles of medium and dark colors

176 B triangles of light colors (mark and cut these in pairs so that you have at least two from each fabric)

Assemble
Lay pieces for each rectangle, face up, to form the design in Fig. 31; B triangles should be from the same fabric. Stitch the B triangles to the A triangle.

Arrange finished rectangles in order, with 25 on each side and 19 for top and bottom border strips. (Be sure all your "geese" are flying clockwise around the quilt.) Join rectangles in each section.

Complete quilt top

After blocks and border strips are pieced and appliquéd, you can put them into rows and border units.

Cut other border pieces
Make templates that are the widths of the borders and about 15" long (you can slide the templates along to mark the required lengths). You'll need two templates—4" wide and 5" wide.

Now find that striped border fabric you set aside earlier. Place templates on the wrong side of the fabric and mark the lengths needed. Cut out the fabric, adding ¼" to ½" seam allowances:

2 strips, 4x75" each, for inner border
2 strips, 4x57" each, for inner border
2 strips, 5x75" each, for outer border
2 strips, 5x57" each, for outer border

Cut sashing
Draft two templates—one 3x15" and one 3" square. To mark the long horizontal strips which go across the quilt, use both templates. On the wrong side of the fabric (along the length), first trace the 3" square. Then butt the 3x15" template against the square and trace it. Move and trace the two templates in this manner until you have a 3x57" length (Fig. 32). Mark 4 more strips in the same way, leaving room for seam allowances between them. The pencil cross marks on each strip will line up with the corners of blocks when you assemble rows.

To mark the vertical sashing strips, use the 3x15" template to trace 16 strips, leaving room for seam allowances.

Cut out all sashing strips, adding ¼" to ½" seam allowances.

Assemble rows
Lay the finished blocks on the floor. Arrange them following the sampler quilt or in another way that pleases you. Lay the sashing pieces between the blocks.

Start at the top and work on one row at a time (Fig. 33). Stitch a vertical sashing strip to the left side of each block (a). Add an extra strip to the block at the right end of the row (b). Stitch the block units together. Then add a long horizontal sashing strip to the top, matching pencil cross marks to corners of the blocks.

On the last row, also add a horizontal sashing strip to the bottom (Fig. 34).

Assemble borders
Lay border pieces and corner blocks in position. The 4"-wide strips form the inner border, with the 4x57" strips at top and bottom. Next are the Wild Goose Chase border strips. (Keep the "geese" headed in the right direction.) On the outside, place the 5"-wide fabric strips.

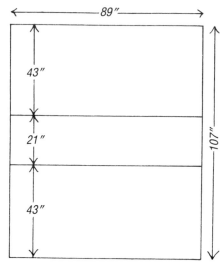

<--- 89" --->

43"

21"

43"

107"

Fig. 35 *Piecing backing (if you quilt the whole top)*

Stitch the three border strips together on all sides to make four border sections. Add a corner appliqué block to both ends of the top and bottom border sections.

Transfer lines for the outside edges of the quilt to the right side of each border section by basting over your pencil lines.

Finish quilt

If you plan to join the top before quilting, see Quilting the whole top, page 149. Stitch the quilt rows together. Add the border sections, first the sides, then the top and bottom. Piece the backing fabric, following Fig. 35.

If you plan to quilt in sections, see Quilting in sections, page 150. Work with the individual rows and border units before stitching them together.

Mark quilting lines

Press the finished top (whole or sections).

Mark lines or designs on the blocks and border pieces listed below. (See *Marking simple lines and shapes,* page 147, and *Marking special designs,* page 148.)

Partridge in a Pear Tree—Mark diagonal lines to crisscross on background; draw first line from corner to corner, then place additional lines 1¾" apart.
Corner appliqué blocks—Mark diagonal lines, following directions above.
American Eagle—Mark center of block with eagle quilting design, page 30.
Dove of Peace—Mark center of block with dove quilting design, page 34.
Birds in Air—On each large off-white triangle, mark a center triangle ¾" from seam lines.
On other blocks with large triangles or squares, you may want to add lines to repeat the shapes, about ¾" from the seam lines.

Quilting guides

Stack the layers, smoothing quilt top over backing and batting. Baste the layers together.

Before you begin stitching, see *Making quilting stitches,* page 148. Quilt blocks and sashing pieces, following guides under *Basic quilting,* page 147. Additional suggestions are below.

Birds in Air—Quilt inside off-white triangles only.
Dove in the Window—On diamonds, quilt inside off-white pieces only (not the doves).
Flying Swallows—Quilt all pieces except the swallows (the groups of three dark diamonds).
Owl—Quilt under the lines of embroidered scallops.
Rooster—Quilt under the lines of embroidered scallops. On upper tail, quilt three evenly spaced lines, following top curve of the tail.
Inside border—Quilt two lengthwise rows. Keep them evenly spaced, following stripes on fabric.
Wild Goose Chase border—Quilt inside the small B triangles only.
Outside border—Quilt three lengthwise rows. Keep them evenly spaced, following stripes on fabric.

Finish edges

Make bias from the 34" square of fabric you saved, and stitch the bias to the quilt. Follow directions under *Using continuous bias,* page 151.

Congratulations!

I hope you enjoyed putting this quilt together as much as I did. It certainly was more challenging than a plain Wild Goose Chase.

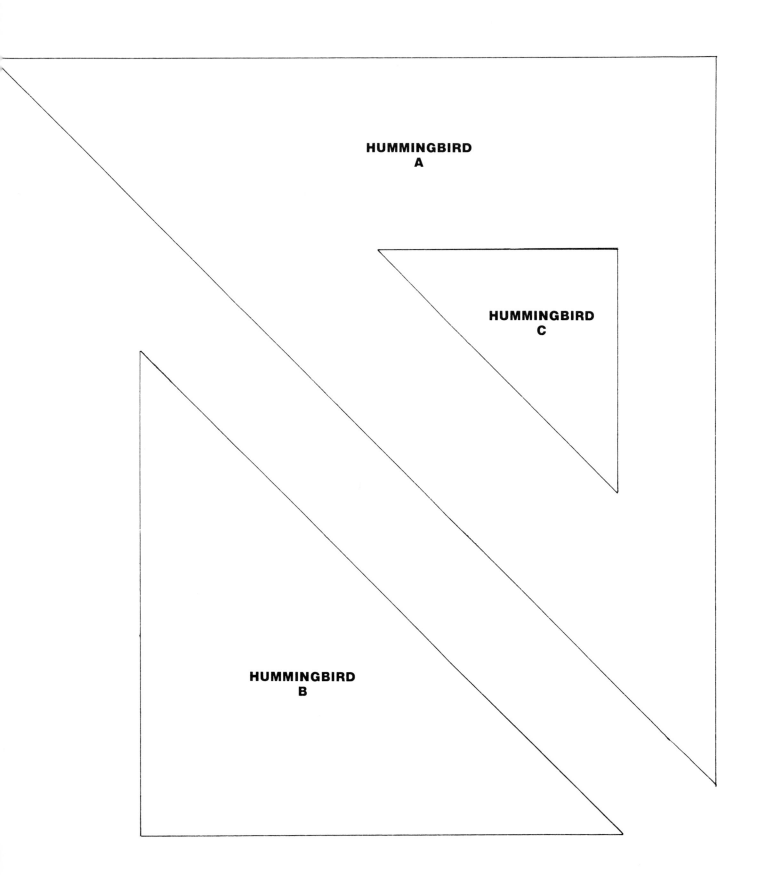

HUMMINGBIRD
A

HUMMINGBIRD
C

HUMMINGBIRD
B

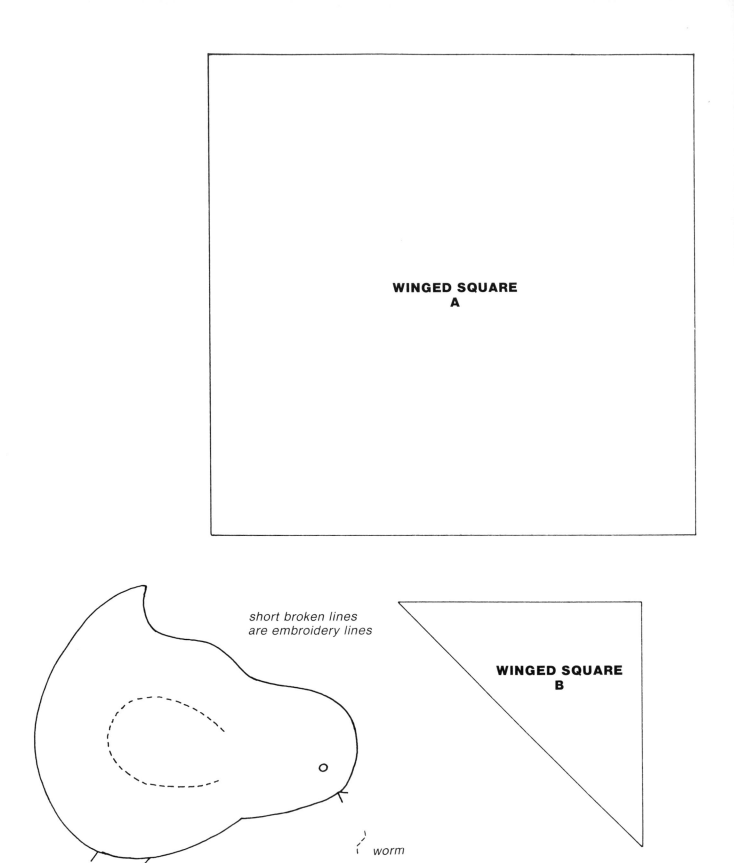

**WINGED SQUARE
A**

*short broken lines
are embroidery lines*

**WINGED SQUARE
B**

worm

**BIRDS
ON THE GROUND**

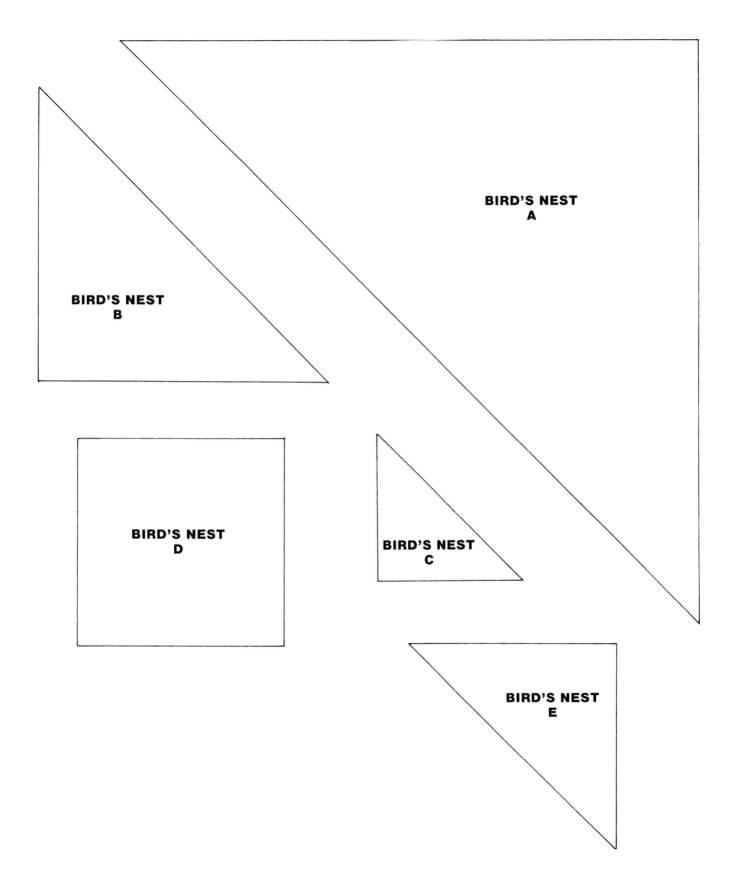

BIRD'S NEST
A

BIRD'S NEST
B

BIRD'S NEST
D

BIRD'S NEST
C

BIRD'S NEST
E

AMERICAN EAGLE
quilting design

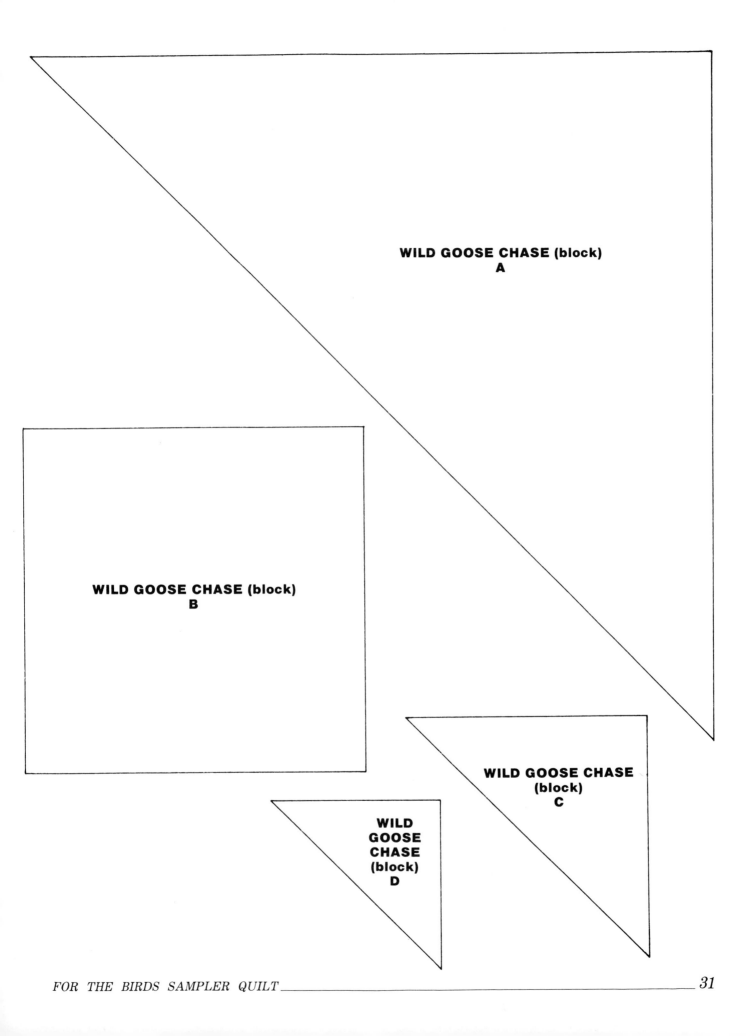

WILD GOOSE CHASE (block)
A

WILD GOOSE CHASE (block)
B

WILD GOOSE CHASE
(block)
C

WILD
GOOSE
CHASE
(block)
D

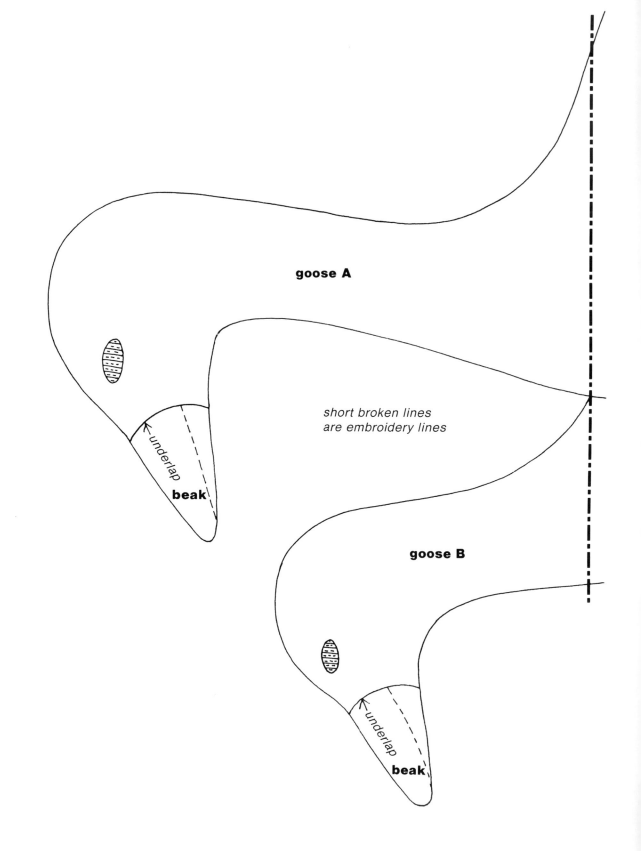

goose A

short broken lines
are embroidery lines

underlap

beak

goose B

underlap

beak

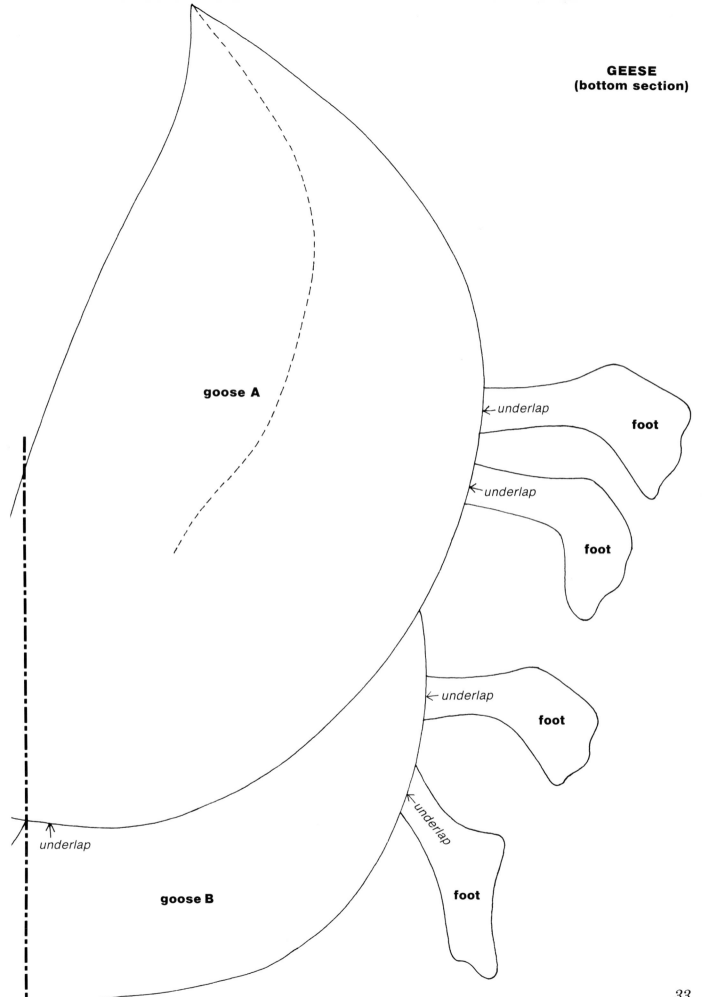

GEESE
(bottom section)

goose A

←underlap

underlap

foot

foot

←underlap

foot

underlap

foot

underlap

goose B

33

DOVE OF PEACE
quilting design

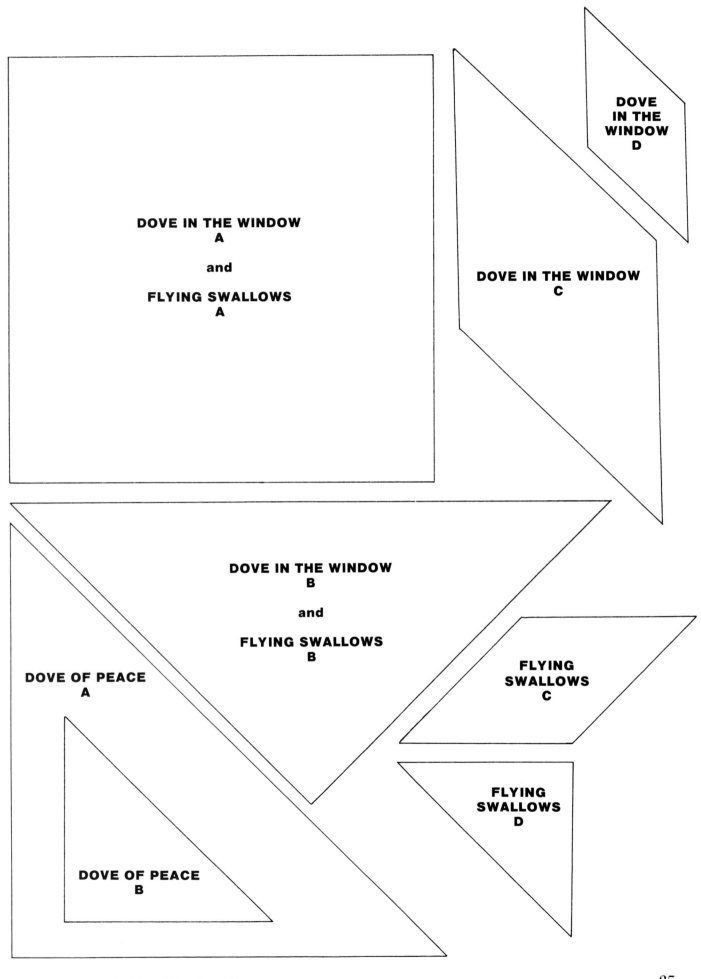

DOVE IN THE WINDOW
A

and

FLYING SWALLOWS
A

DOVE
IN THE
WINDOW
D

DOVE IN THE WINDOW
C

DOVE IN THE WINDOW
B

and

FLYING SWALLOWS
B

DOVE OF PEACE
A

DOVE OF PEACE
B

FLYING
SWALLOWS
C

FLYING
SWALLOWS
D

OWL
(top section)

short broken lines are embroidery lines

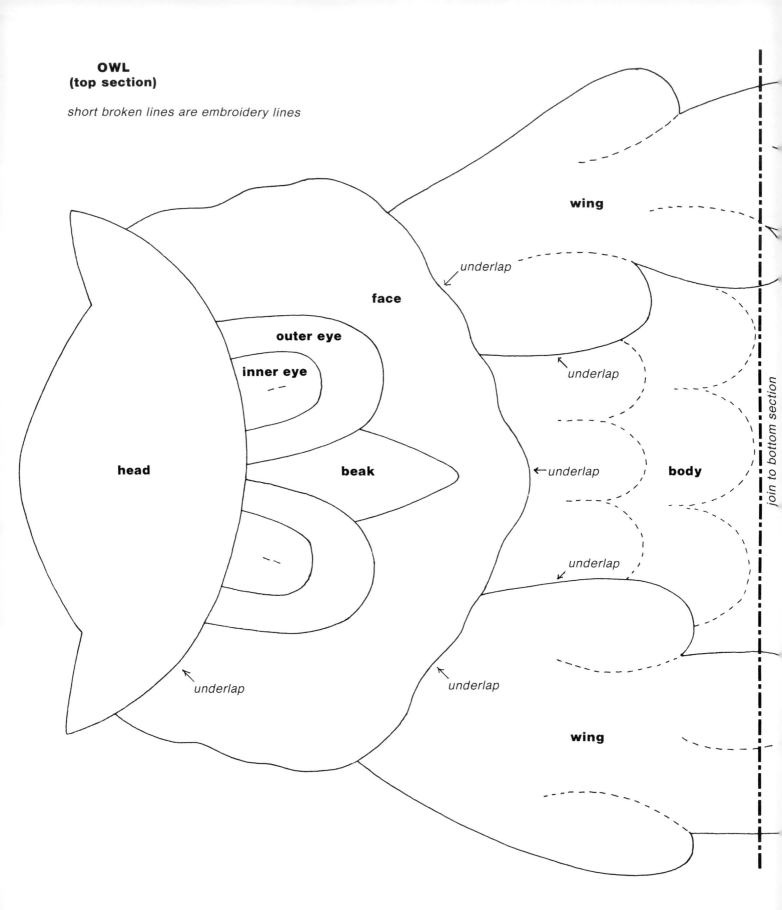

wing

underlap

face

outer eye

underlap

inner eye

underlap

body

head

beak

underlap

underlap

underlap

join to bottom section

underlap

underlap

wing

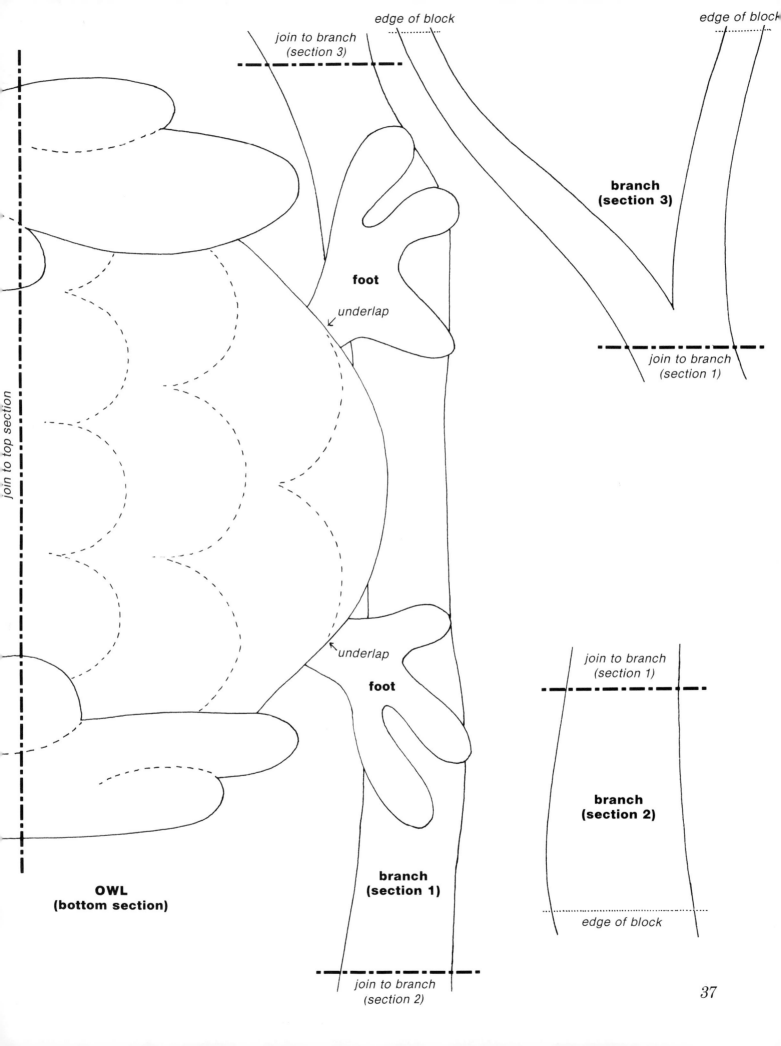

edge of block

join to branch
(section 3)

edge of block

branch
(section 3)

foot

underlap

join to branch
(section 1)

join to top section

underlap

foot

join to branch
(section 1)

branch
(section 2)

OWL
(bottom section)

branch
(section 1)

edge of block

join to branch
(section 2)

37

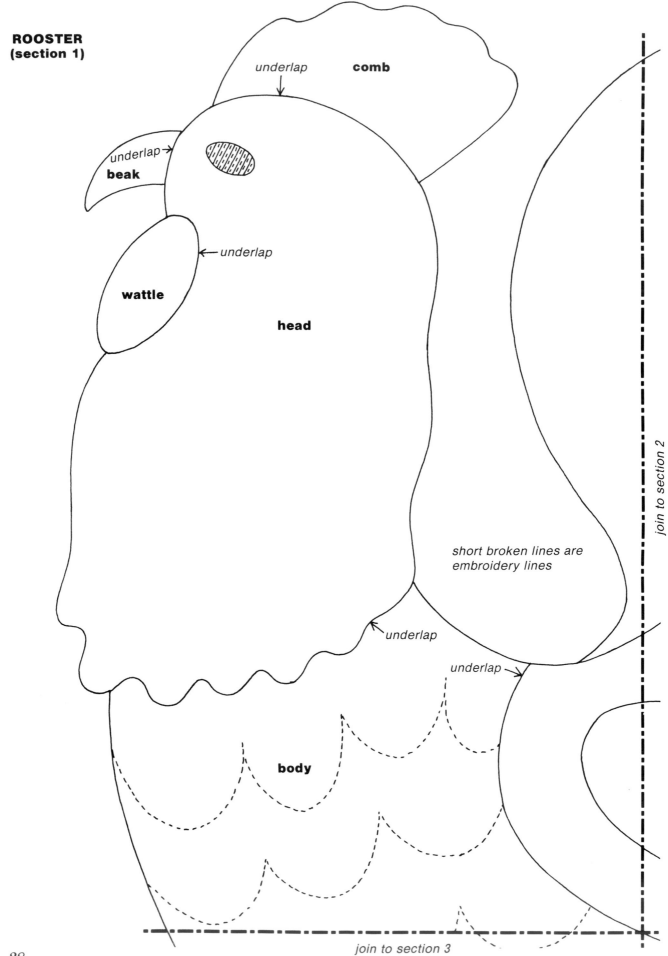

ROOSTER
(section 1)

comb

underlap

underlap →

beak

← *underlap*

wattle

head

short broken lines are embroidery lines

← *underlap*

underlap →

body

join to section 2

join to section 3

38

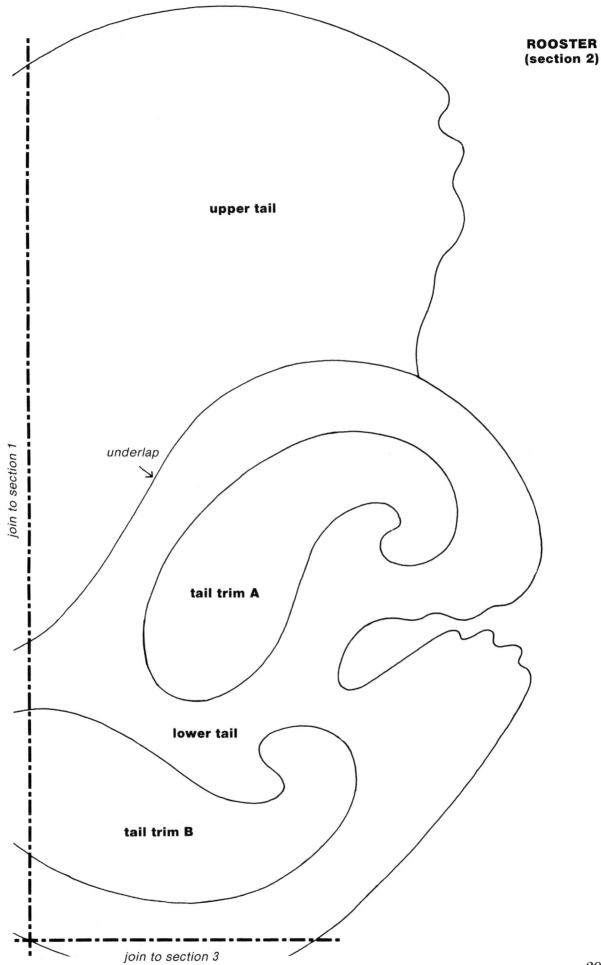

upper tail

underlap

tail trim A

join to section 1

lower tail

tail trim B

join to section 3

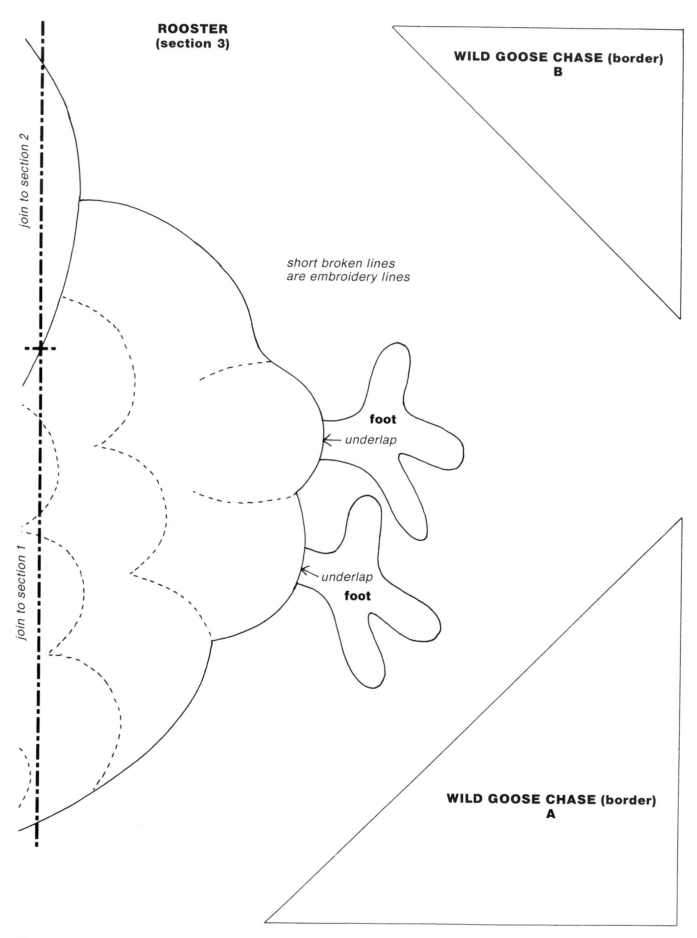

ROOSTER
(section 3)

WILD GOOSE CHASE (border)
B

join to section 2

short broken lines
are embroidery lines

foot
← underlap

join to section 1

← underlap
foot

WILD GOOSE CHASE (border)
A

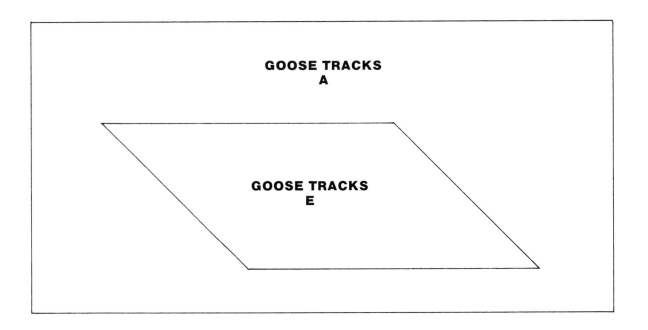

**GOOSE TRACKS
A**

**GOOSE TRACKS
E**

**GOOSE TRACKS
B**

**GOOSE TRACKS
C**

**GOOSE TRACKS
D**

**BIRDS IN AIR
B**

**BIRDS IN AIR
A**

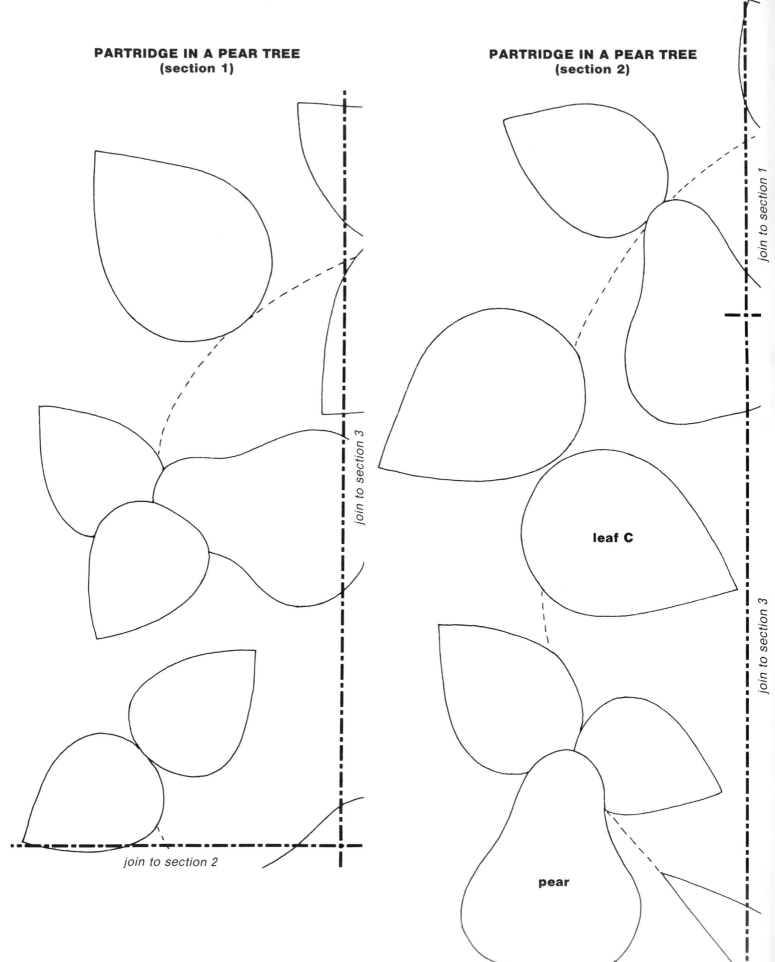

PARTRIDGE IN A PEAR TREE
(section 1)

PARTRIDGE IN A PEAR TREE
(section 2)

join to section 3

join to section 2

join to section 1

join to section 3

leaf C

pear

42

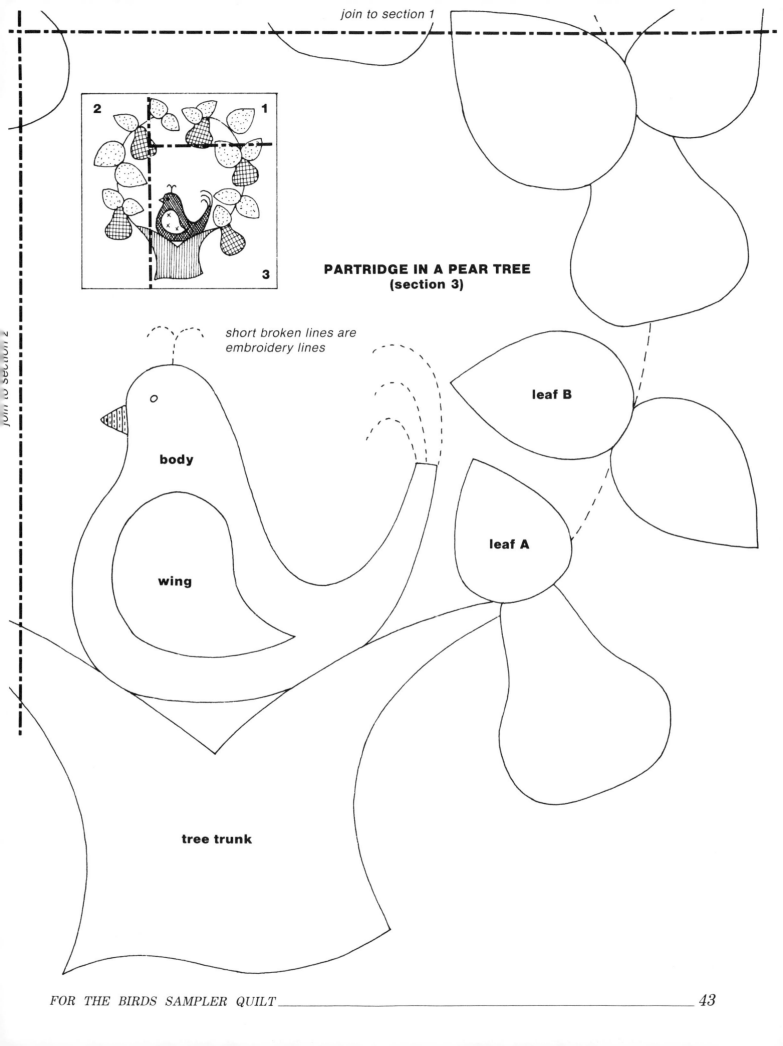

join to section 2

PARTRIDGE IN A PEAR TREE
(section 3)

short broken lines are
embroidery lines

leaf B

body

leaf A

wing

tree trunk

(color photo, page 50)

3 Christmas Sampler Quilt

It's fun to bring out a special quilt for the holidays, and this is one you can leave on display all year if you like. There is no Santa Claus or reindeer, and the red and green colors are toned down by the prints (there is a little black in both prints).

This quilt was made to satisfy a request from one of my "Christmas in July" classes. The women wanted something more challenging than the usual patchwork ornaments. They suggested starting a quilt in July and finishing it by Christmas.

I began to hunt for quilt blocks that related to Christmas—and was surprised to find there were so few. I used what I could, filled in with other blocks and even designed a few appliqués of my own.

There are 13 different blocks in the quilt. The center section has seven pieced blocks and five appliquéd blocks. A pieced Pine Tree is used at all four corners.

All the blocks are 15" square, so they can be switched around. You could omit one design and repeat one you like better (or that is easier to make).

In my For the Birds quilt, I used a Partridge in a Pear Tree appliqué (page 23). This block also is 15" square, and you could include it in your Christmas quilt.

In spite of my habit of using many fabrics, I managed to limit myself to three prints and one solid color for this quilt. The same fabrics are repeated in various blocks, sashing, borders and bias binding. The backing is a red print.

You can sew the whole top together before quilting, or you can quilt in sections. You may want to read about the two methods in Chapter 12 before you begin.

The finished quilt is 87x105".

Materials
(Yardage is for fabric 45" wide.)

3½ yd. red print
3½ yd. green print
2½ yd. off-white print
2 yd. off-white solid
7½ yd. print or solid, for backing, if you plan to assemble the whole top before quilting (*or* 10 yd., if you plan to quilt in sections)
Thread for piecing in white or blending color
Thread for appliqué in matching colors
Quilting thread in off-white or colors
Embroidery floss in off-white, green, gold, black (red is optional)
Polyester batting: 1 pkg. 90x108", if you plan to assemble the whole top before quilting (*or* 1 pkg. 90x108" and ½ pkg. 72x90", if you plan to quilt in sections)

Prepare fabric

Prewash all the fabric if you plan to wash the finished quilt. Then cut off sections which will be used later for making sashing, borders and background squares.

From red print, cut 1⅓ yd. for sashing. Also cut a section 32x76" along the length for border pieces.

From the green print, cut 1⅓ yd. From this section, cut a 34" square for making bias binding, and save the rest for the corner sashing squares.

From the green print, also cut a 16x76" section along the length for border pieces.

From the off-white print, cut a 24x76" section along the length for border pieces.

Set these print sections aside, and use remaining lengths for making the quilt blocks.

To be sure you have enough fabric to cut background squares, cut a 32x48" section from the off-white solid. Use remainder for piecing the blocks that follow.

Make each block

For tips on making templates, piecing blocks and doing appliqué, see Chapter 1.

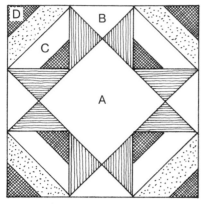

Fig. 1 **NIGHT AND NOON**
(color photo, page 13)

Fig. 2 *Piecing corner square*

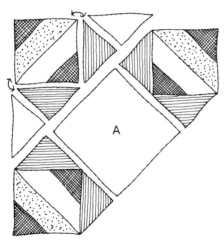

Fig. 3 *Forming corner triangle and center row*

Fig. 4 **ROSE WREATH**
(color photo, page 13)

NIGHT AND NOON

Let's begin by piecing the relatively simple block in Fig. 1. That big center square won't look so plain after you've filled it with quilting.

Make templates

Trace patterns A-D, pages 60-61, and make templates. (The crystal quilting design for A can be copied later.)

Cut fabric

Place templates on the wrong side of the fabric and trace. Cut out, adding ¼" to ½" seam allowances:

1 A square of off-white solid
8 B triangles of red print
4 B triangles of off-white solid
4 C shapes of off-white solid
4 C shapes of off-white print
8 D triangles of green print

Assemble

Lay all pieces, face up, to form the block in Fig. 1. Begin with a corner (Fig. 2). Pin-baste and stitch pieces together, matching pencil lines and end points. Trim each seam and finger-press to the darker side. Complete the three other corners and put the square units back in position.

Work with the upper left corner square (Fig. 3). Add two red B triangles, then two off-white B triangles. Repeat step with lower right corner square. There you go—you have two large corner triangles.

Now work with the remaining corner squares, first adding red B triangles and then joining the units to center A square (Fig. 3). When you place this long piece back in the line-up, you have three diagonal rows.

Finish block by joining the rows, carefully matching intersecting seams with pins.

ROSE WREATH

Now let's do some appliqué. The wreath in Fig. 4 has eight red print flowers separated by eight green print leaves.

Make templates

Trace patterns for flower, flower center and leaf, page 62, and make templates. Also draft a 15" square for the background fabric. (Save this big template for other appliqué blocks.)

Cut fabric

Place the rose template, face up, on the right side of the red print. Trace 8 roses and cut out the fabric, adding ¼" seam allowances.

To cut and form the flower centers and leaves, follow directions for *Making perfect circles*, page 7. You will need:

8 flower centers of off-white solid
8 leaves of green print

Place the 15"-square template on the wrong side of the off-white solid and trace. Cut out fabric, adding ¼" to ½" seam allowances.

Assemble

Stay-stitch each rose (optional) and clip seam allowance into the V points. Turn seam allowance, baste and press.

To find center of background square, fold fabric into quarters and finger-press. Open fabric, and position roses in a circle. Have four centered on the fold lines and four others in between. Roses should just touch. Pin in place.

Position a leaf where two roses meet, tucking one end under the flowers.

Now take those perfect off-white circles and center one on each rose. If the red fabric shows through, cut a liner of off-white fabric or batting. Liner should be just a bit smaller than the flower center (with no

(continued on page 51)

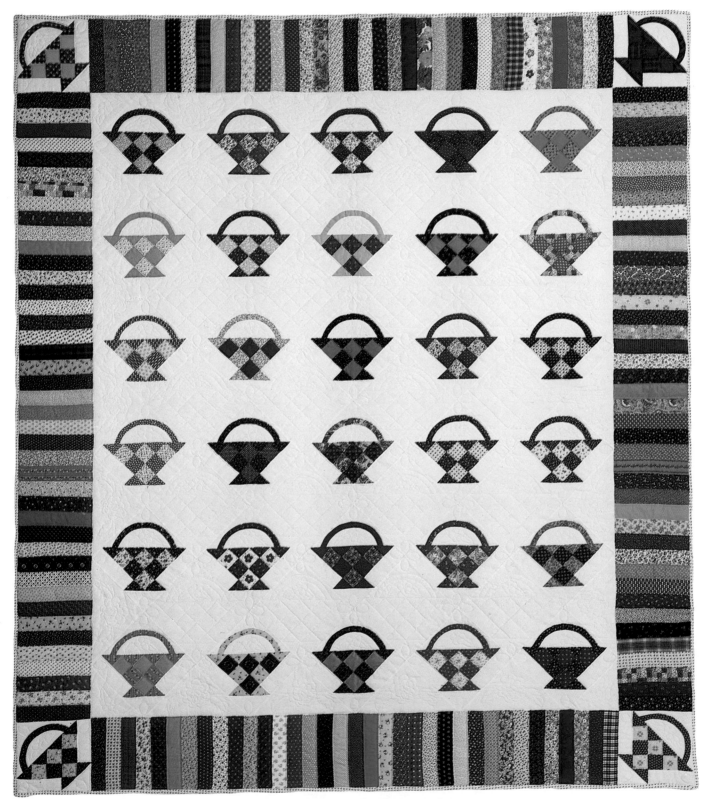

Scrap Basket Quilt, page 97

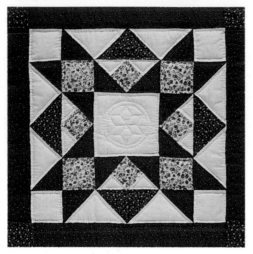

Christmas Star, page 51

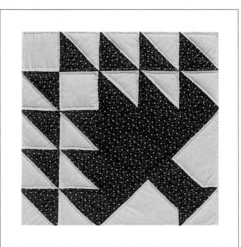

Pine Tree, page 51

Holly Wreath, page 52

Poinsettia, page 53

Christmas Rose, page 54

Birds in the Tree, page 54

Christmas Basket, page 55

Carpenter's Wheel, page 56

Star of Bethlehem, page 56

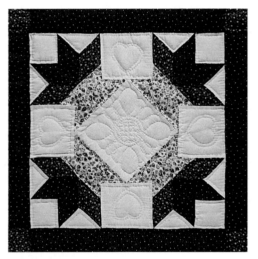

Christmas Cactus, page 57

Hexagon Wreath, page 57

Maiden's Delight, page 77

Christmas Sampler Quilt

_____ *LET'S MAKE MORE PATCHWORK QUILTS*

15½" block 36 pg. "grid"

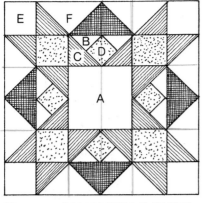

Fig. 5 ***CHRISTMAS STAR***
(color photo, page 48)

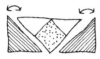

Fig. 6 *Piecing rectangle*

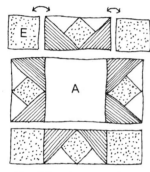

Fig. 7 *Piecing center square*

Fig. 8 *Piecing outside rectangles*

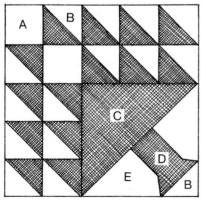

Fig. 9 ***PINE TREE***
(color photo, page 48)

(continued from page 46)

seam allowance). Place liner against the wrong side of the flower center, under the seam allowance.

Sew pieces to background, using matching thread and the appliqué stitch (page 8).

CHRISTMAS STAR

Here's another pieced block, with a few more pieces than Night and Noon. It's called Christmas Star.

Make templates
Trace patterns A-F, page 61, and make templates.

Cut fabric
Place templates on the wrong side of the fabric and trace. Cut out, adding ¼" to ½" seam allowances:

   1 A square of off-white solid
   8 B triangles of off-white solid
  16 C triangles of red print
   4 D squares of off-white print
   4 E squares of off-white print
   4 E squares of off-white solid
   4 F triangles of green print
   8 F triangles of off-white solid

Assemble
Lay all pieces, face up, to form the block in Fig. 5. Begin by stitching two B triangles to adjacent sides of a D square, making a larger triangle (Fig. 6). Add a C triangle at each end to make a rectangle.

Repeat steps to complete the same rectangle on all four sides of the block (surrounding square A).

Add an off-white print E square to each end of the top rectangle (Fig. 7). Repeat for bottom row of block.

Join remaining two rectangles to sides of square A.

Now you can work with rows. Stitch the three horizontal rows together to make the inner square.

Stitch an off-white F triangle to the sides of a green print F triangle (Fig. 8). Then add a C triangle to each end. Repeat steps to complete three more rectangles.

Add an off-white E square to each end of the top and bottom rows (see Fig. 5). Stitch the side rectangles to the inner square—and we're back to rows. Now, stitch the top and bottom rows to the center section to complete the block.

PINE TREE

There is a Pine Tree block at each corner of the quilt, so you will need four of these. The blocks are turned in different directions, but they're all pieced in the same way, and you'll find them fairly easy to put together. Directions are given for making one block.

Make templates
Trace patterns A, B, D and E, page 63. Also trace half pattern for C to make a full C pattern. To do this, fold paper in half, then open paper and place fold over broken line. Trace half the triangle, refold paper and trace other half to complete the triangle.

Make templates for all the patterns.

Cut fabric
Place templates on the wrong side of the fabric and trace. Cut out, adding ¼" to ½" seam allowances:

   2 A squares of off-white solid
  15 B triangles of off-white solid
  14 B triangles of green print
   1 C triangle of green print
   1 D shape of green print
   1 E shape of off-white solid
   1 E (reversed) of off-white solid

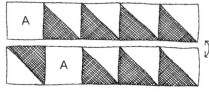

Fig. 10 *Piecing top section*

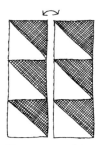

Fig. 11 *Piecing side section*

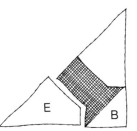

Fig. 12 *Piecing corner triangle*

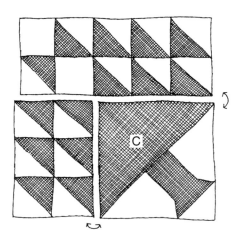

Fig. 13 *Completing block*

Assemble

Before you lay the pieces in front of you as usual, take the 14 green print B triangles and pin an off-white B triangle to each one along the diagonal. Make sure the pencil lines and end points match.

If you use a machine, feed the triangles, a pair at a time, under the presser foot to stitch the diagonal seams. Don't cut the thread between the pairs until you are done—you'll have a wonderful kite tail.

Now, cut the pairs apart and finger-press the seams to the dark side. Wonderful! You have 14 squares and are ready to line up all the pieces, face up, to form the block in Fig. 9.

Start with the off-white square A in the top row and stitch the row together. Stitch the second row together, noting the position of the print triangle in the first square. Then join the two rows (Fig. 10). There, you have the top section!

Next work with the three squares that form a vertical row on the left, and stitch the squares together. Repeat with the next vertical row of squares. Then sew the two vertical rows together (Fig. 11). Another section!

For the third section, sew the off-white B triangle to the bottom of green print D (Fig. 12). Make sure that the E's are positioned correctly (one is cut reversed). To join one E to the D, stitch from the bottom edge to the point where D turns. Stop, backstitch and remove fabric from machine. Clip the seam allowance almost to the turning point (this will let the fabric spread for the turn). Pin the two pieces together from the turning point to the top, and stitch. Repeat the step for the other side to complete a triangle.

Now sew the triangle you have just made to the big C triangle (Fig. 13). Add the second section (to the left of the square), then the top section.

And there's your Pine Tree. "Now," I whisper, "make three more."

HOLLY WREATH

Holly leaves and little red berries form this wreath. You can attach the leaves with a regular appliqué stitch or make a decorative embroidery stitch with green floss. A compass is helpful for drawing a large circle guideline.

Make templates

Trace patterns for leaf and berry, page 62, and make templates. (You can use a nickel for the berry, if you like.) You'll also need a 15"-square template for the background fabric.

Now take a good look at the leaf template. "All those points and curves," you may say. "Am I really going to turn and baste 15 leaves?"

A lot of people who have made this quilt say, "Sure." Others say, "No way." So they cut the leaves with no seam allowances, and attach them with green embroidery floss and a buttonhole stitch to cover the raw edges. (See *buttonhole stitch*, page 9.)

Yes, I know you may have a horror of raw edges, but if you make a neat, close buttonhole stitch, the wreath will look fine.

If you can't decide, try a leaf each way—one with a seam allowance turned and appliquéd in the usual way, and one with no seam allowance, attached with a buttonhole stitch.

Cut fabric

When you're ready, place the leaf template on the right side of the green print and trace 15 times. Cut out (adding 1/4" seam allowances if you plan to turn under the raw edges).

Place the berry template (or a nickel) on the right side of the red print and trace 29 times.

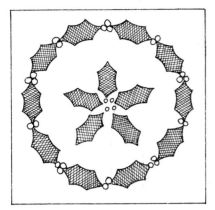

Fig. 14 *HOLLY WREATH*
(color photo, page 48)

Fig. 15 *POINSETTIA*
(color photo, page 48)

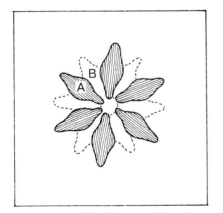

Fig. 16 *Placing appliqués*

Cut out the circles—right on the pencil lines. (These raw edges will be hidden.)

Place the 15″-square template on the wrong side of the off-white solid and trace. Cut out fabric, adding ¼″ to ½″ seam allowances.

Assemble

If you added seam allowances to the leaves, stay-stitch (optional) and slash seam allowances along the inside curves. Turn the seam allowances, baste and press.

If you did not add seam allowances, the leaves are ready to appliqué.

To find the center of the background square, fold the fabric into quarters and finger-press. Open fabric, and use a compass to lightly draw an 11″ circle (5½″ radius).

Lay 10 of the leaves around the circle, spacing them so they almost meet. By eye, place the remaining five leaves so they radiate from the center, making a five-pointed star; leave a little space in the center for the holly berries. Pin in place.

Sew leaves to background square. If you have turned under seam allowances, you can use the appliqué stitch (page 8) and matching thread—or you can work a blanket stitch (page 9) with green embroidery floss.

If you have raw edges, use a close buttonhole stitch (page 9) and green embroidery floss.

Now for those holly berries. For each berry, make a running stitch around the edge of the fabric circle. Draw thread, gathering the edge until you have a plump little ball. Flatten the fabric with your finger, hiding the raw edge underneath. There you are—a holly berry.

Make 29 berries. Position four in the center of the block, and pin two or three where leaves meet around the circle. Appliqué with red thread.

POINSETTIA

There are three templates for this pretty appliquéd block. I know the red parts are really bracts, but I'm going to call them petals.

Make templates

Trace patterns for petals A and B and for the leaf, page 62, and make templates. Also use a 15″-square template for the background fabric.

Cut fabric

Place appliqué templates on the right side of the fabric and trace. Cut out, adding ¼″ seam allowances:

    6 A petals of red print
    6 B petals of red print

To cut and form the leaves, follow directions for *Making perfect circles*, page 7. You will need 12 leaves of green print.

Place the 15″-square template on the wrong side of the off-white solid and trace. Cut out, adding ¼″ to ½″ seam allowances.

Assemble

Stay-stitch each petal (optional) and slash seam allowances along inside curves. Turn seam allowances, baste and press.

To find the center of the background square, fold the fabric into quarters and finger-press. Open fabric and arrange the petals, with large ones on top and small ones underneath (Fig. 16). Leave a space in the middle for embroidering gold French knots.

Arrange leaves at random around the outside, tucking them under the petals. Pin appliqués in place.

Sew pieces to background, using matching thread and the appliqué stitch (page 8). Begin with the bottom layers.

To finish the center of the poinsettia, use three strands of gold embroidery floss and make French knots (page 9).

Fig. 17   CHRISTMAS ROSE
(color photo, page 48)

Fig. 18   BIRDS IN THE TREE
(color photo, page 48)

CHRISTMAS ROSE

This large flower is cut from one piece of fabric and is appliquéd with a blanket stitch. All those petals are formed with lines of embroidery.

Make templates

Trace pattern for leaf, page 64, and make a template. Trace pattern for rose, pages 64-65, joining sections on broken lines and copying all the design lines. Do not make a template. You also will need a 15"-square template for the background.

Cut fabric

Place your rose tracing on the right side of the red print fabric, and slip a piece of dressmaker's carbon (white or yellow) between the layers. With a used-up ball-point pen (one with no ink), trace all the lines of the rose onto the fabric. Peek under the carbon to make sure the lines are showing up on the red fabric. Good—it worked!

Cut out the rose, adding a ¼" seam allowance.

To cut and form the leaves, follow directions for *Making perfect circles*, page 7. You will need 12 leaves of green print.

Place the 15"-square template on the wrong side of the off-white solid and trace. Cut out, adding ¼" to ½" seam allowances.

Assemble

Stay-stitch rose (optional) and slash seam allowance into the V points and inside curves. Turn seam allowance, baste and press.

Center rose on background square; then pin the 12 leaves around the outside. Tuck end of each leaf under rose.

Attach leaves, using green thread and the appliqué stitch (page 8). To attach rose, use two strands of off-white embroidery floss and the blanket stitch (page 9).

To embroider inner lines on rose, use two strands of off-white floss and the chain stitch (page 9). Begin at the center and work to the outside.

Now wasn't that easy?

BIRDS IN THE TREE

This is an adaptation of a very old block seen on some historical quilts, and it combines appliqué with embroidery. I used the same design on my For the Birds Sampler quilt.

Make templates

Read directions for *Picture Appliqués*, page 8, before you begin. Then trace the pattern, pages 65-67, joining the three sections on broken lines. Transfer the tracing to a 15" square of poster board. This will be your whole template.

Cut fabric

Place the whole template, face down, on the wrong side of the off-white solid. Tape template to fabric, and trace around the outside edges to mark seam lines. With template still in place, cut out fabric, adding ¼" to ½" seam allowances.

Turn fabric over—you should be able to see the design through the fabric. Very lightly, copy all the lines with a sharp No. 5H or 6H pencil.

Now you can cut apart the whole picture to make individual templates—tree trunk, bird bodies, heads, wings and leaves. Since all leaves are different, you may want to cut them out and prepare the fabric one at a time.

Place templates, face up, on the right side of the fabric and trace. Cut out, adding ¼" seam allowances:

    1 tree trunk of off-white print
    2 bird bodies of green print
    2 bird heads of red print
    2 bird wings of red print
To cut and form the 14 small leaves, use green print and

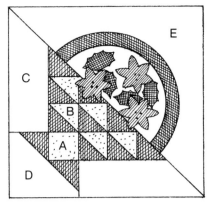

Fig. 19 *CHRISTMAS BASKET*
(color photo, page 49)

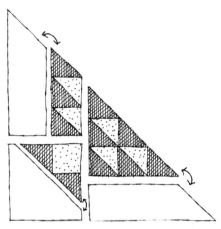

Fig. 20 *Piecing basket triangle*

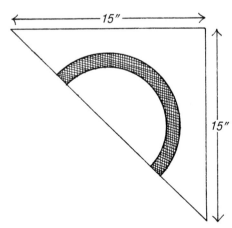

Fig. 21 *Appliquéing handle*

follow directions for *Making perfect circles,* page 7.

Assemble

Stay-stitch appliqué pieces (optional) and slash seam allowances into V points and inside curves. Turn seam allowances (unless they tuck under another piece), baste and press.

Position appliqué pieces on the background fabric, using your pencil lines as a guide. Pin in place.

Sew pieces to background fabric, beginning with the bottom layers. You can use matching thread and the appliqué stitch (page 8), or floss with an embroidery stitch. For my sampler quilt, I attached the tree trunk with green embroidery floss and a blanket stitch (page 9).

Embroider leaf stems with green floss and the chain stitch (page 9). For beaks, use black floss and the satin stitch (page 9). For eyes, use black floss and French knots (page 9).

CHRISTMAS BASKET

Red print flowers spill out of a pieced basket. You can attach the flowers and leaves with an appliqué stitch or with an embroidery stitch.

Make templates

Trace patterns A–D, page 68, and for basket handle, flower and leaf, page 69. Make templates.

Also draft a large E triangle on poster board. Draw 15" lines on two sides of a square corner (see Fig. 21). Connect these lines with a diagonal, and cut out the triangle.

Cut fabric

Place templates for pieced work on the wrong side of the fabric and trace. Cut out, adding ¼" to ½" seam allowances:
    1 A square of off-white print

    5 B triangles of off-white print
    11 B triangles of green print
    1 C shape of off-white solid
    1 C (reversed) of off-white solid
    1 D shape of off-white solid
    1 E triangle of off-white solid

Place appliqué templates on the right side of the fabric and trace. Cut out, adding ¼" seam allowances:
    1 handle of green print
    3 flowers of red print
    4 leaves of green print

Set appliqué pieces aside until block is pieced.

Assemble

Pin a green print B triangle to each of the 5 off-white print B triangles to make squares. Stitch the seams, trim and finger-press to the dark side.

Lay all the pieces, face up, to form the block in Fig. 19. Sew pieces together to form units, then sew units together to form the basket triangle (Fig. 20).

For handle, stay-stitch curves (optional) and slash seam allowance along the inside curve. Turn seam allowances on curves to wrong side, baste and press. Center handle on the E triangle (Fig. 21). Raw edges of handle ends will be even with raw edges of triangle. Sew in place with matching thread and the appliqué stitch (page 8).

Stitch the two large triangles together to form the block.

To prepare appliqués, stay-stitch around each piece (optional) and slash seam allowances into V points and inside curves. Turn seam allowances, baste and press.

Position flowers and leaves on the block, following Fig. 19 as a guide.

To attach appliqués, you can use matching thread and the appliqué stitch (page 8), or embroidery floss and a blanket stitch (page 9).

Embroider the center of each flower with gold floss and a few French knots (page 9).

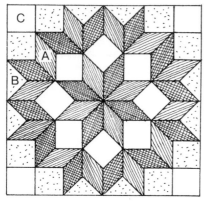

Fig. 22 CARPENTER'S WHEEL
(color photo, page 49)

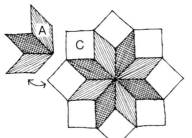

Fig. 23 *Adding a trio of diamonds*

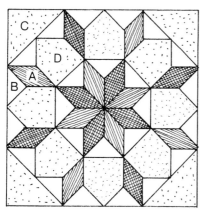

Fig. 24 STAR OF BETHLEHEM
(color photo, page 49)

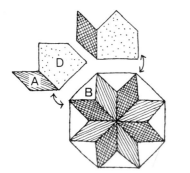

Fig. 25 *Working with units*

CARPENTER'S WHEEL

This pieced block—and the next two—have diamonds, so please read the tips on *Piecing diamonds,* page 4, before you begin. Because the pieces are so small, some people find it easier to do the sewing by hand instead of by machine.

Make templates

Trace patterns A-C, page 70, and make templates. (Note that patterns A and B also are used for Star of Bethlehem.)

Cut fabric

Place templates on the wrong side of fabric and trace. Cut out, adding ¼″ to ½″ seam allowances:

    16 A diamonds of green print
    16 A diamonds of red print
     8 B triangles of off-white print
    12 C squares of off-white solid
     8 C squares of off-white print

Assemble

Lay all pieces, face up, to form the block in Fig. 22. Join the center star of eight diamonds—four green print and four red print. Remember to stitch only from pencil point to pencil point; do not stitch into seam allowances. Then add eight off-white solid C squares to the star, stitching each square in two steps.

Join the remaining diamonds in groups of three, as shown in Fig. 23. Fit each unit into place and stitch in two steps. Sew adjoining diamond units together to close the ring.

Add off-white print triangles and squares. Finally, fill in the corners with off-white solid squares.

Look! You've just turned 60 little pieces of fabric into one striking quilt block.

STAR OF BETHLEHEM

Here's another block with diamonds. It also has many small pieces, so you may want to do the stitching by hand. Refer to the tips on *Piecing diamonds,* page 4.

Make templates

Trace patterns A-D, page 70, and make templates. (Note that patterns A and B also are used for Carpenter's Wheel.)

Cut fabric

Place templates on wrong side of fabric and trace. Cut out, adding ¼″ to ½″ seam allowances:

     8 A diamonds of red print
     8 A diamonds of green print
    24 B triangles of off-white solid
     4 C triangles of off-white print
     8 D shapes of off-white print

Assemble

Lay all pieces, face up, to form the block in Fig. 24. Assemble the center star of eight diamonds—four red print and four green print; do not stitch into seam allowances.

Add eight off-white B triangles between the diamond points, stitching each triangle in two steps.

Make units of an A and a D by sewing a diamond to the left side of each D shape (Fig. 25). Watching the color arrangement, sew each A/D unit to a B triangle. Then carefully sew the free edge of each D piece to the adjoining A diamond.

Piece in the remaining B triangles. Finally, add a C triangle to each corner, and the block is completed.

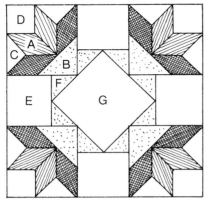

Fig. 26 *CHRISTMAS CACTUS*
(color photo, page 49)

Fig. 27 *Piecing a corner*

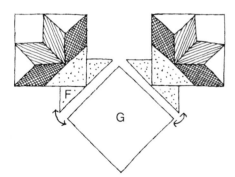

Fig. 28 *Adding center of block*

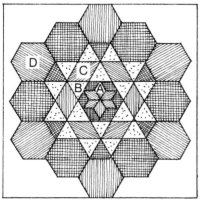

Fig. 29 *HEXAGON WREATH*
(color photo, page 49)

CHRISTMAS CACTUS

An old block called Cactus Basket inspired this design. I put four of the blocks together, eliminated some seams, and named it Christmas Cactus.

Be sure to review the tips on *Piecing diamonds*, page 4.

Make templates
Trace patterns A-G, pages 70-71, and make templates.

Cut fabric
Place templates on the wrong side of the fabric and trace. Cut out, adding ¼" to ½" seam allowances:

    8 A diamonds of green print
    8 A diamonds of red print
    4 B triangles of off-white print
    8 C triangles of off-white solid
    4 D squares of off-white solid
    4 E rectangles of off-white solid
    8 F triangles of off-white print
    1 G square of off-white solid

Assemble
Lay all pieces, face up, to form the block in Fig. 26. The flower in each corner has two red diamonds between two green diamonds.

Begin each corner unit by joining the four diamonds (Fig. 27); do not stitch into seam allowances. Piece in the C triangles and a D square. Then add a B triangle.

To form each basket, join an F triangle to both sides of the B triangle (Fig. 28). Stitch only from pencil point to pencil point; do not stitch into the seam allowances.

Sew a cactus basket to each side of the G square. Yes, I know—now you have open spaces.

Position an E rectangle in each opening, and stitch it in three steps; do not stitch into

seam allowances at the inside corners.

That completes Christmas Cactus—and there's only one quilt block left.

HEXAGON WREATH

Hexagons mean English piecing, with paper templates and hand sewing, and most people love it. For Hexagon Wreath, you piece the large design, then appliqué it to a background square.

Please read all about *English piecing*, page 6, before you begin.

Make templates
For exact piecing, you'll need to cut a paper template for every fabric piece in the design. Trace patterns B, C and D, page 72, and make poster board or plastic templates. Then, on typing-weight paper, trace the master templates and cut out:

    24 B triangles
    6 C diamonds
    12 D hexagons

To make templates for the A diamonds that form the center star, place a piece of typing-weight paper directly over the pattern on page 72. Carefully trace the whole star and the surrounding diamonds. Cut the 12 A diamonds apart, and use these for your piecing. (I've found this is the best way to keep the exact shape of the small A diamonds. When people trace them from a master template, the diamonds seem to "grow," and the finished star is too big for the block.)

Now find the 15"-square template that you've been using to mark the background fabric.

Cut fabric
Pin the paper templates to the wrong side of the fabric. Cut out around them, adding at least ¼" seam allowances. (Do

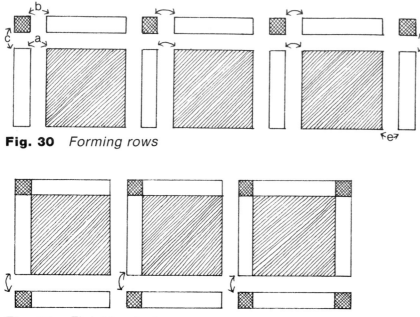

Fig. 30 *Forming rows*

Fig. 31 *Finishing last row*

not remove templates.) You will need:

- 6 A diamonds of red print
- 6 A diamonds of green print
- 18 B triangles of off-white print
- 6 B triangles of green print
- 6 C diamonds of red print
- 6 D hexagons of red print
- 6 D hexagons of green print

To prepare the small pieces, fold the fabric over the paper and baste through the paper.

Place the 15"-square template on the wrong side of the off-white solid and trace. Cut out, adding ¼" to ½" seam allowances.

Assemble

Lay all pieces, face up, to form the design in Fig. 29. Begin with the red center diamonds and join them with a whipping stitch (page 6) to form a star. Use the same stitch to add the green diamonds that surround the star. Continue piecing in the same manner until the whole wreath is finished.

Before you pop the papers, press the wreath so the outside edges will stay turned under. Now snip and remove all the bastings, and the papers will pop right out!

Center the finished wreath on the off-white background square and pin. Attach with thread in matching colors and the appliqué stitch (page 8).

Complete quilt top

After the blocks are pieced and appliquéd, you can stitch them into rows and make the borders.

Cut sashing

Draft a template 3x15" (for strip), and another 3" square (for corners). Place templates on the wrong side of the fabric and trace. Cut out, adding ¼" to ½" seam allowances:

- 31 strips, 3x15" each, of red print
- 20 squares, 3x3" each, of green print

Assemble rows

Lay the finished quilt blocks and sashing pieces on the floor and arrange them in rows (Fig. 30). Start at the top and work on one row at a time. Sew one sashing strip to the left side of each block (a). Above each block, add a green square to the end of a sashing strip (b), then sew this unit to the top of each block (c).

At the right end of the row, add a green square to the top of a sashing strip (d), and stitch the unit to the end block (e). Finally, join the block units to form a horizontal row.

Repeat steps for all rows. *Note*: On the last row, also add sashing units to the bottom of each block (Fig. 31) before joining the block units.

Cut border pieces

You'll need templates that are the widths of the borders and about 15" long (you can slide the templates along to mark the required lengths). Use your 3x15" sashing template, and make two more—5" wide and 7" wide.

Place templates on the wrong side of the fabric and mark the lengths needed. Cut out, adding ¼" to ½" seam allowances:

- 2 off-white print strips, 5x75" each, for inner border
- 2 off-white print strips, 5x57" each, for inner border
- 2 green print strips, 3x75" each, for middle border
- 2 green print strips, 3x57" each, for middle border
- 2 red print strips, 7x75" each, for outside border
- 2 red print strips, 7x57" each, for outside border

Assemble borders

Lay border pieces and Pine Tree blocks in position, following photo on page 44. The 75" lengths are along each side, and the 57" lengths are at the top and bottom.

For each border section, stitch the three border strips together. Add a Pine Tree block to both ends of the top and bottom sections.

Pencil lines on the red border strips mark the outside edges of the quilt. Baste over these lines to transfer them to the quilt top.

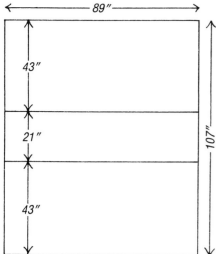

Fig. 32 *Piecing the backing (if you quilt the whole top as one unit)*

Fig. 33 *Using triangle template to create diamonds*

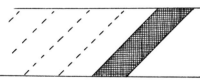

Fig. 34 *Using template to mark diagonal lines*

Fig. 35 *Reversing template to create diamonds*

Finish quilt

If you plan to join the top before quilting, see Quilting the whole top, page 149. Stitch the quilt rows together. Add the border units, first the sides, then the top and bottom. Piece the backing fabric, following Fig. 32.

If you plan to quilt in sections, see Quilting in sections, page 150. Work with the individual rows and border units before stitching them together.

Mark quilting lines

Press the finished top (whole or sections).

Mark lines or designs on the blocks and border pieces listed below. (See *Marking simple lines and shapes*, page 147, and *Marking special designs*, page 148.)

Rose Wreath—Mark diagonal lines to crisscross on the background; draw first line from corner to corner, then place additional lines 1¾" apart.
Christmas Basket—Mark diagonal lines on background, following directions above.
Christmas Rose—Make templates for three leaf quilting designs, page 65. Mark the background with overlapping leaf pattern; draw center (vein) line for each leaf.
Hexagon Wreath—Use hexagon template to mark each corner.
Night and Noon—Mark center of block with crystal quilting design, page 60.
Christmas Star—Mark center of block with star quilting design, page 61.
Christmas Cactus—Mark center of block with the swirl quilting design, page 71. Mark each E shape with the heart quilting design, page 71.
White print border—Make template for border quilting pattern A, page 73. Place long side of the triangle on each edge of border to mark lines; this will form diamonds (Fig. 33).

Red print border—Make template for border quilting pattern B, page 73. Use template to mark diagonal lines (Fig. 34). Then reverse template to mark diagonal lines in opposite direction, forming diamonds (Fig. 35).

Quilting guides

Stack the layers, smoothing quilt top over backing and batting. Baste the layers together.

Before you begin stitching, see *Making quilting stitches*, page 148. Quilt blocks and sashing pieces, following guides under *Basic quilting*, page 147. Also quilt lines and designs you have marked. Additional suggestions are below.

Pine Tree—Quilt large section of tree as one unit.
Rose Wreath—Quilt around each white flower center, and up the center of each leaf.
Poinsettia—Quilt part way up the center of each petal and leaf.
Christmas Basket—Quilt pieced basket inside the white print pieces only (not the green pieces).
Christmas Birds—Quilt under each bird head and around each wing.
Green print border—Quilt along each seam line.

Finish edges

Make bias from the 34" square of green print, and stitch bias to the quilt. Follow directions under *Using continuous bias*, page 151.

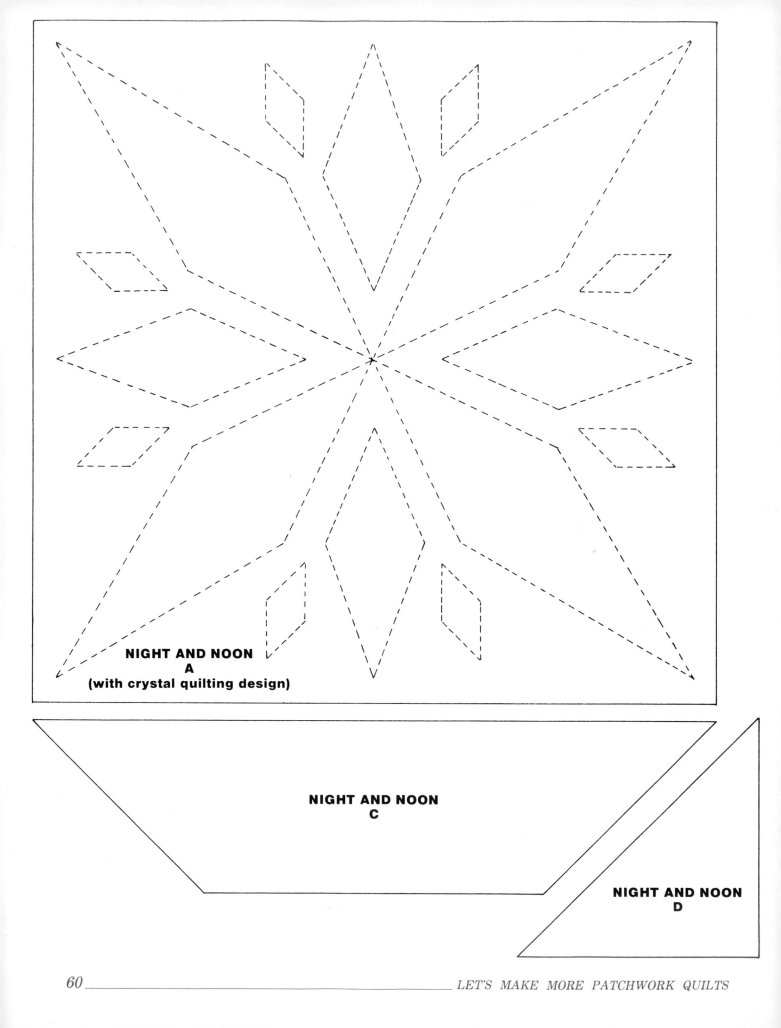

**NIGHT AND NOON
A
(with crystal quilting design)**

**NIGHT AND NOON
C**

**NIGHT AND NOON
D**

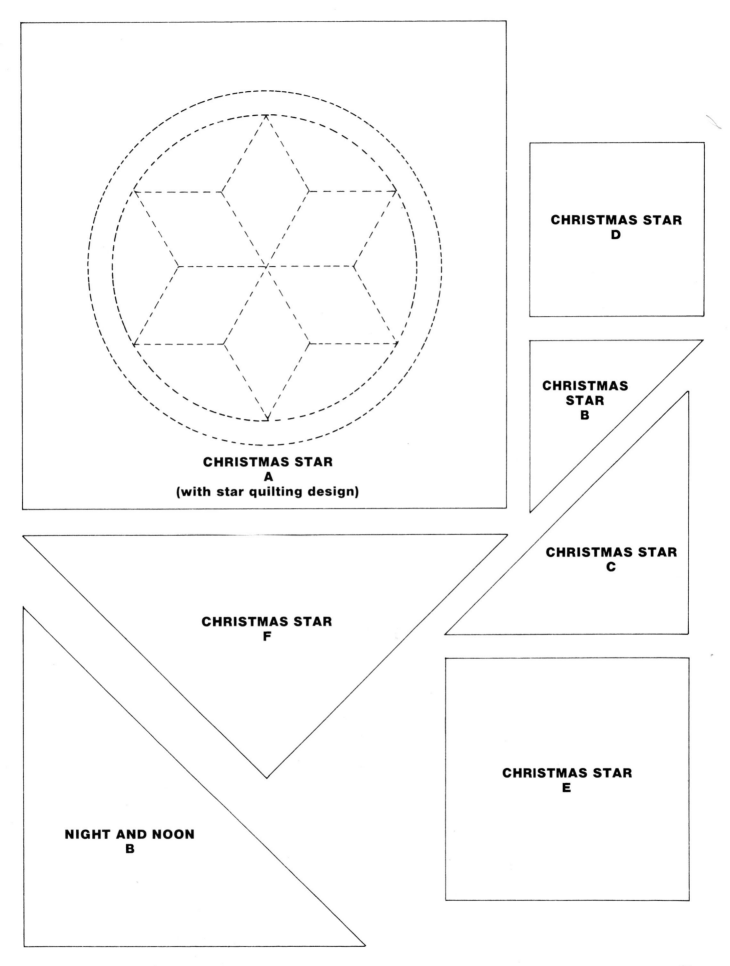

CHRISTMAS STAR
D

CHRISTMAS
STAR
B

CHRISTMAS STAR
A
(with star quilting design)

CHRISTMAS STAR
C

CHRISTMAS STAR
F

CHRISTMAS STAR
E

NIGHT AND NOON
B

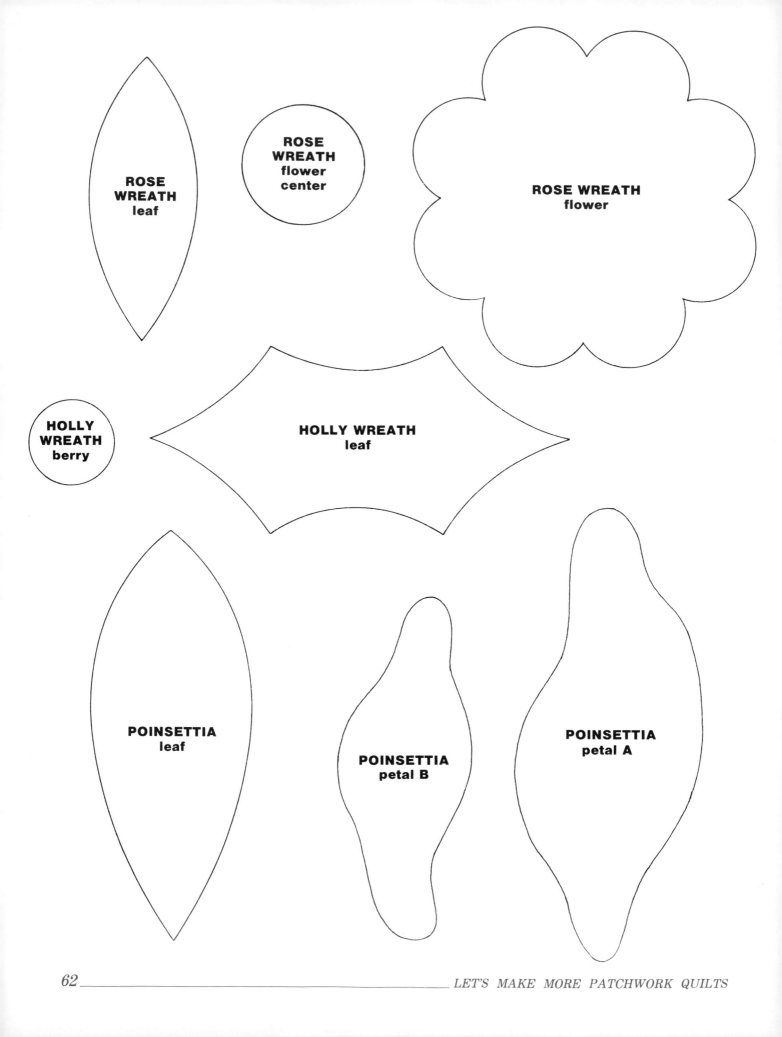

ROSE
WREATH
leaf

ROSE
WREATH
flower
center

ROSE WREATH
flower

HOLLY
WREATH
berry

HOLLY WREATH
leaf

POINSETTIA
leaf

POINSETTIA
petal B

POINSETTIA
petal A

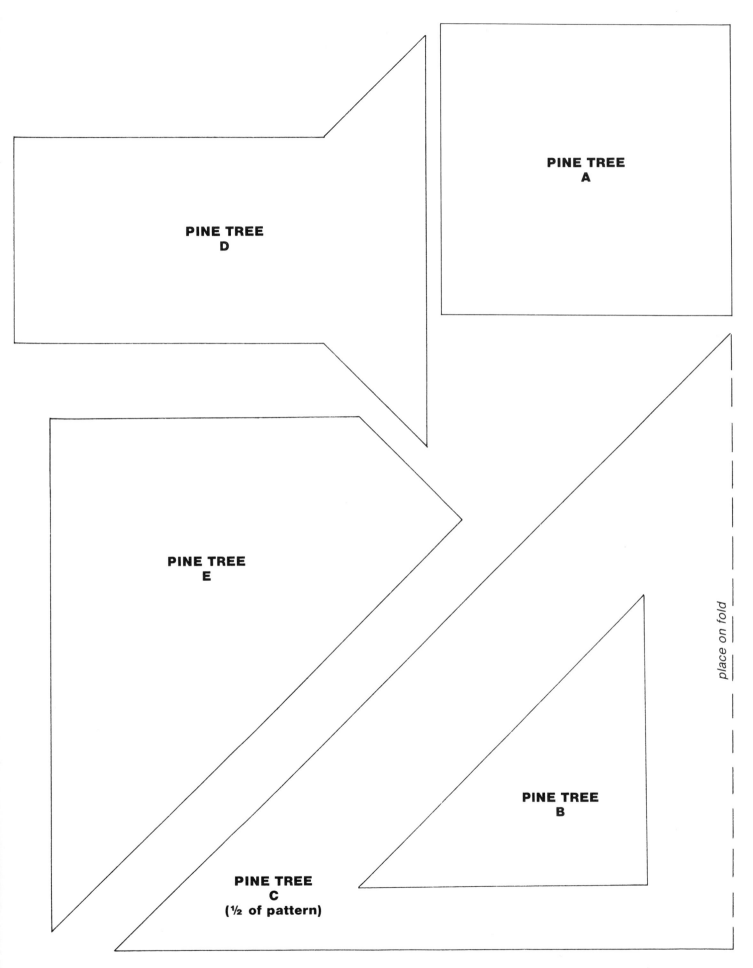

PINE TREE
A

PINE TREE
D

PINE TREE
E

PINE TREE
B

PINE TREE
C
(½ of pattern)

place on fold

**CHRISTMAS ROSE
(left section)**

*short broken lines are
embroidery lines*

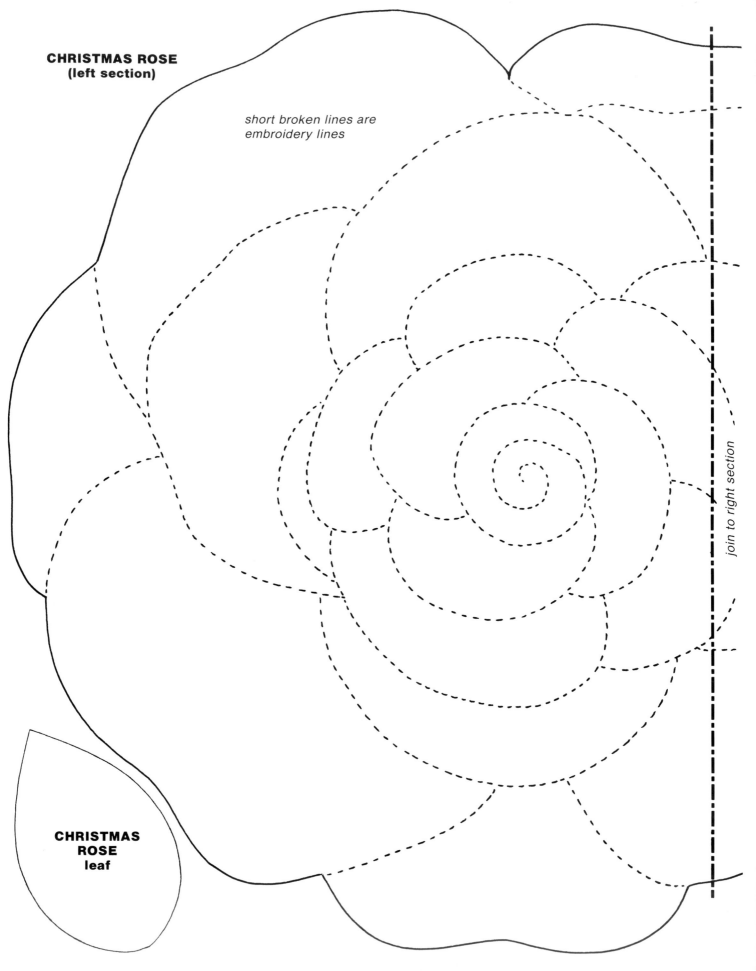

join to right section

**CHRISTMAS
ROSE
leaf**

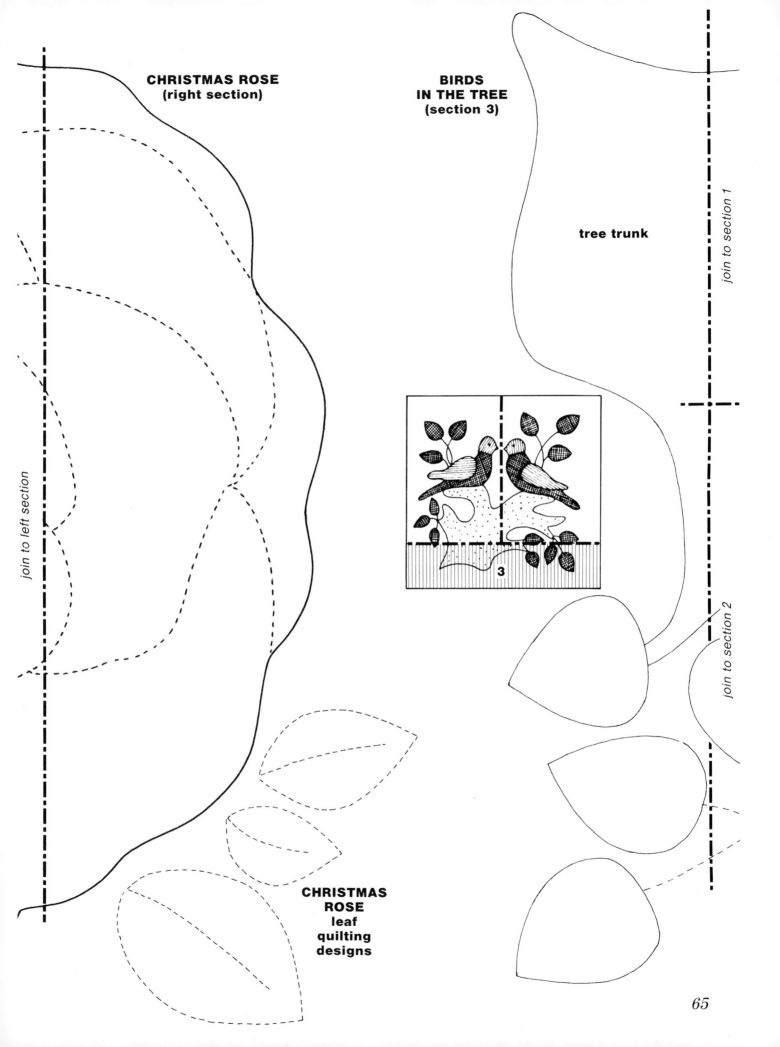

CHRISTMAS ROSE
(right section)

**BIRDS
IN THE TREE
(section 3)**

tree trunk

join to section 1

join to left section

3

join to section 2

**CHRISTMAS
ROSE
leaf
quilting
designs**

65

BIRDS IN THE TREE
(section 1)

*short broken lines are
embroidery lines*

head A

underlap

wing A

body A

tree trunk

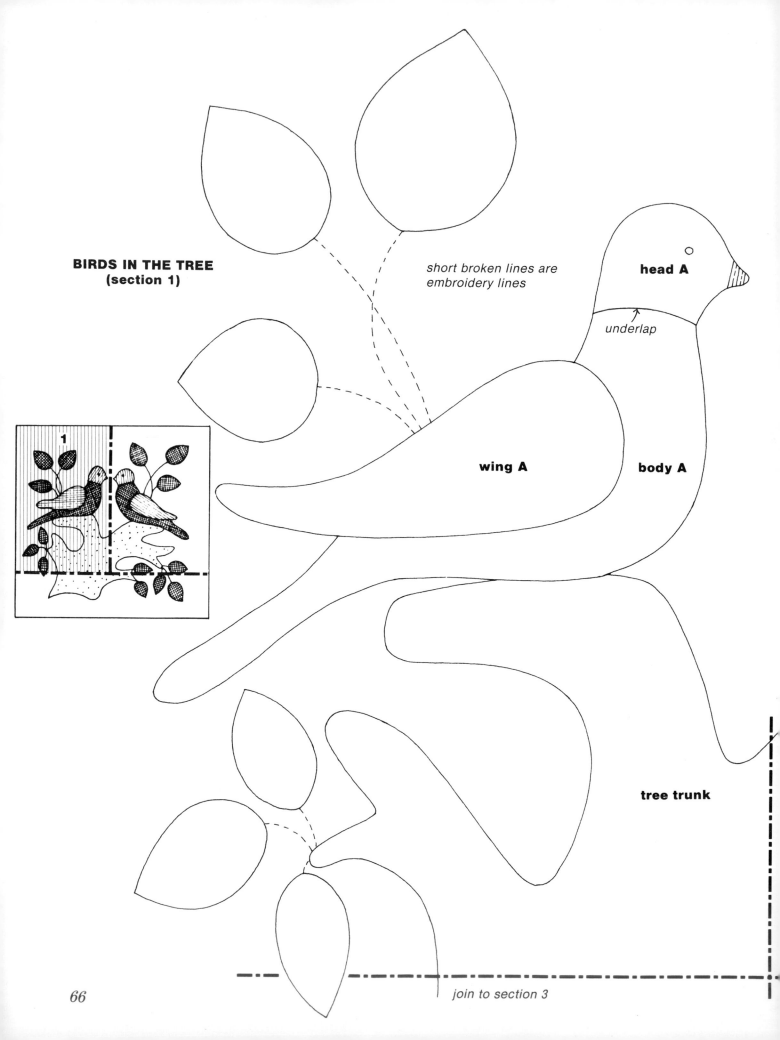

join to section 3

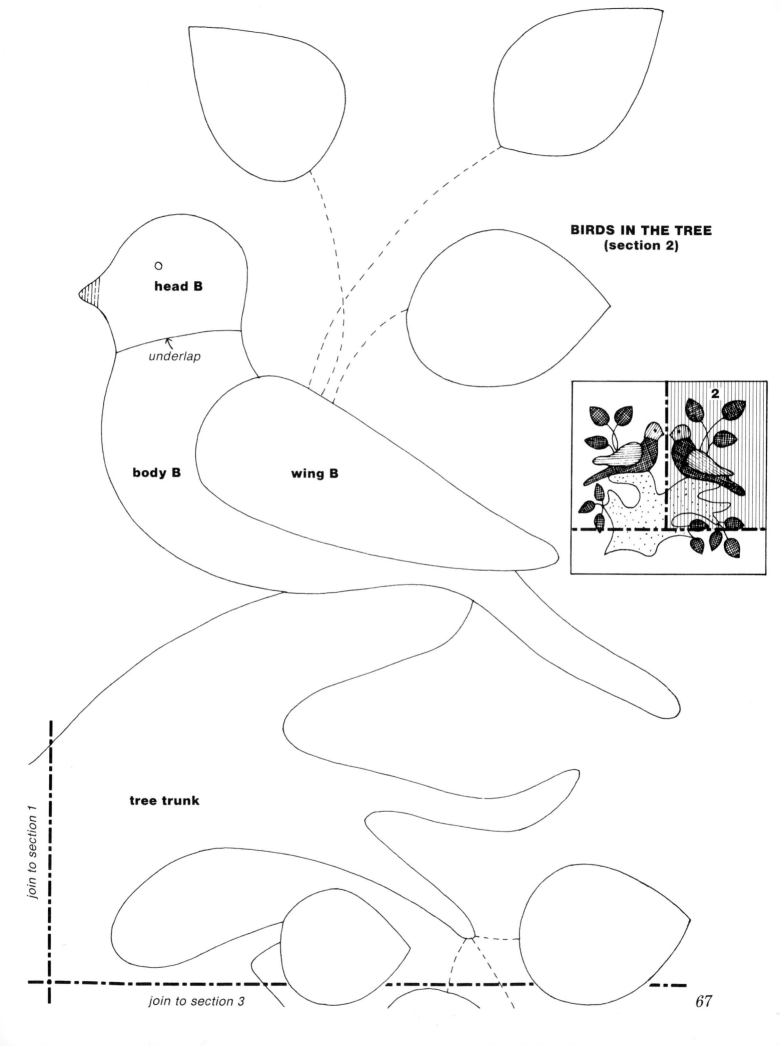

head B

○

BIRDS IN THE TREE
(section 2)

underlap

body B

wing B

tree trunk

join to section 1

join to section 3

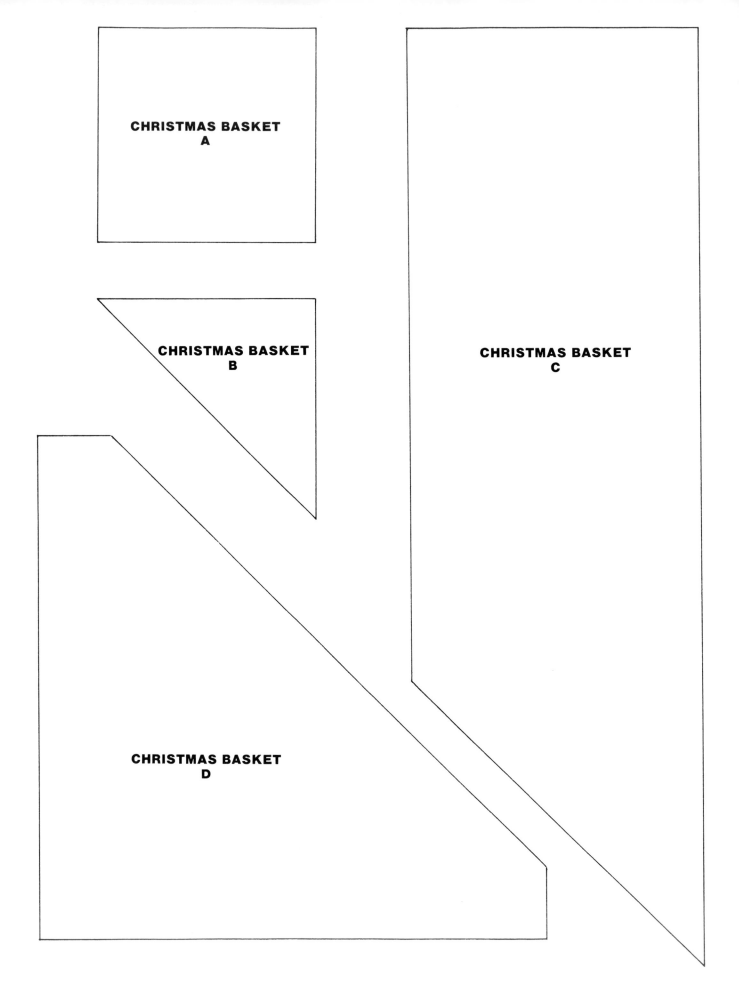

**CHRISTMAS BASKET
A**

**CHRISTMAS BASKET
B**

**CHRISTMAS BASKET
C**

**CHRISTMAS BASKET
D**

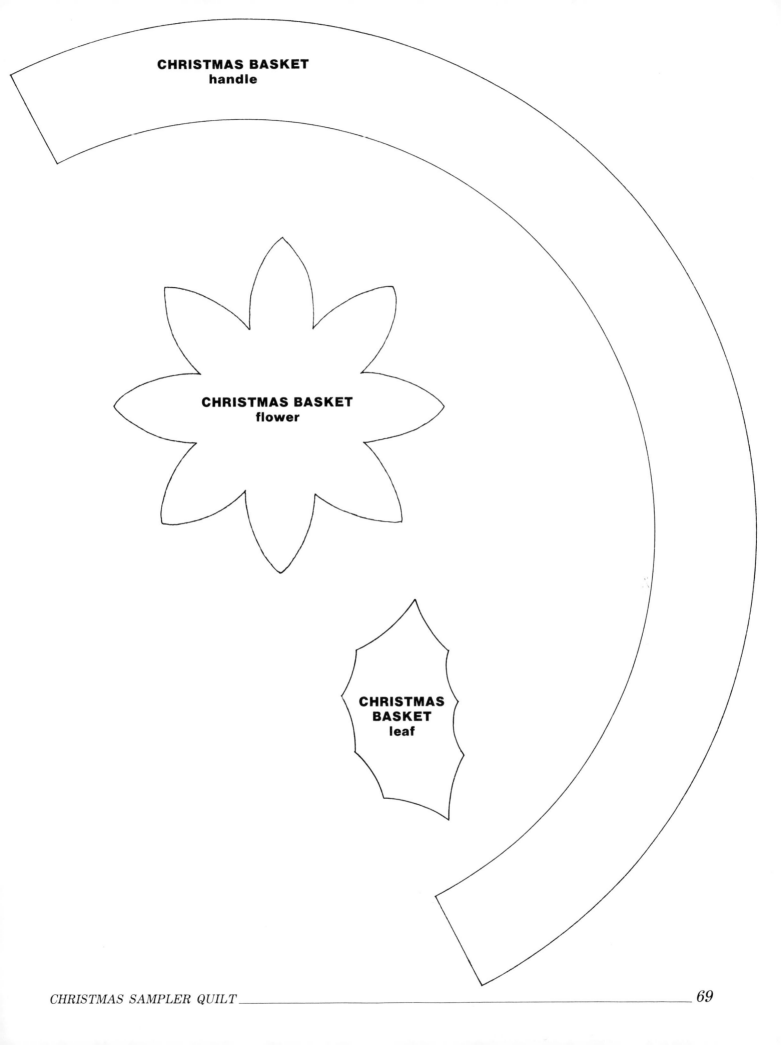

CHRISTMAS BASKET
handle

CHRISTMAS BASKET
flower

CHRISTMAS BASKET
leaf

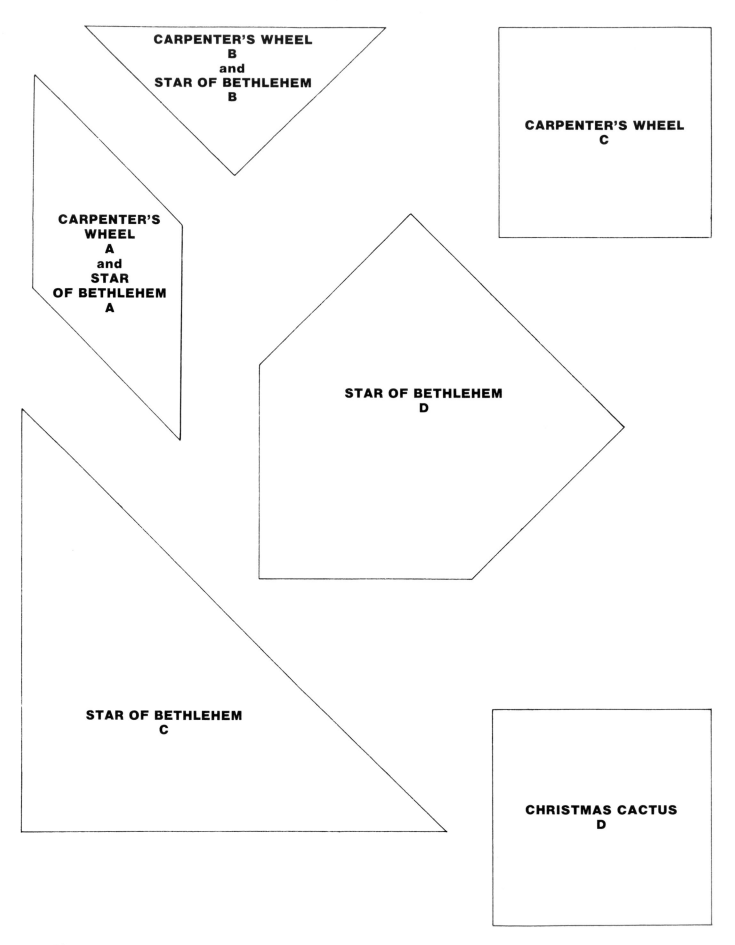

CARPENTER'S WHEEL
B
and
STAR OF BETHLEHEM
B

CARPENTER'S WHEEL C

CARPENTER'S
WHEEL
A
and
STAR
OF BETHLEHEM
A

STAR OF BETHLEHEM
D

STAR OF BETHLEHEM
C

CHRISTMAS CACTUS
D

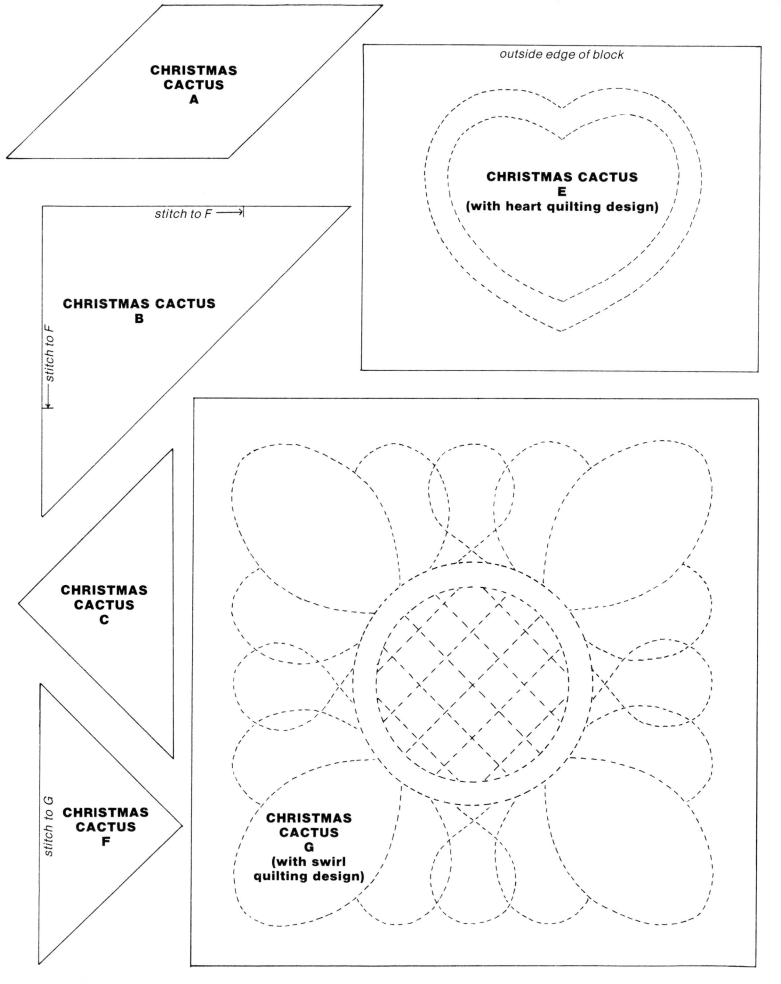

CHRISTMAS CACTUS A

stitch to F →

CHRISTMAS CACTUS B

stitch to F

CHRISTMAS CACTUS C

stitch to G

CHRISTMAS CACTUS F

outside edge of block

CHRISTMAS CACTUS E (with heart quilting design)

CHRISTMAS CACTUS G (with swirl quilting design)

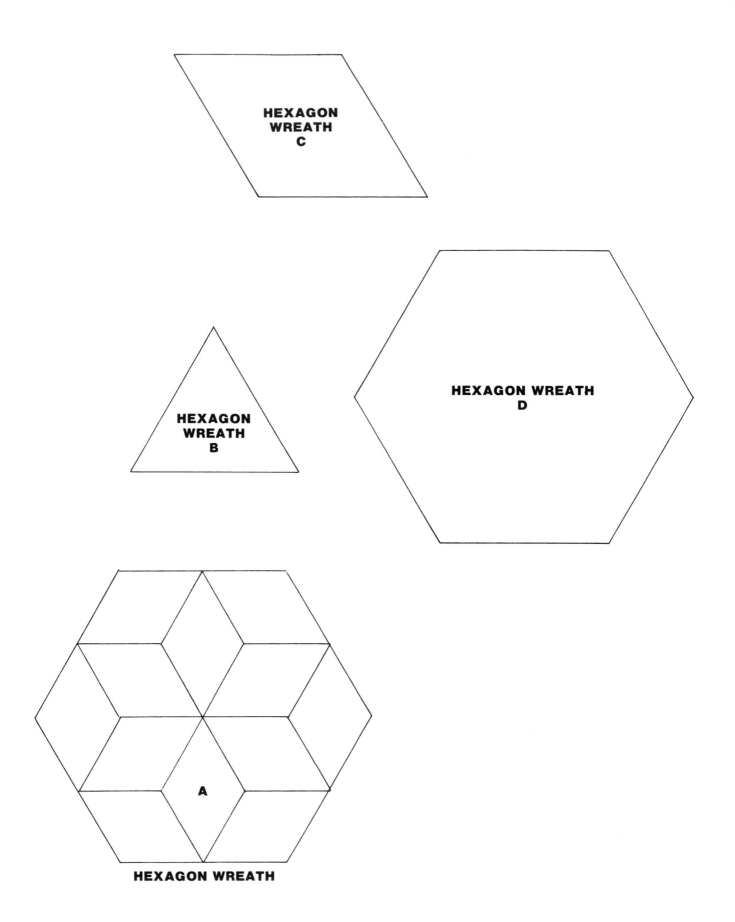

HEXAGON WREATH
C

HEXAGON
WREATH
B

HEXAGON WREATH
D

A

HEXAGON WREATH

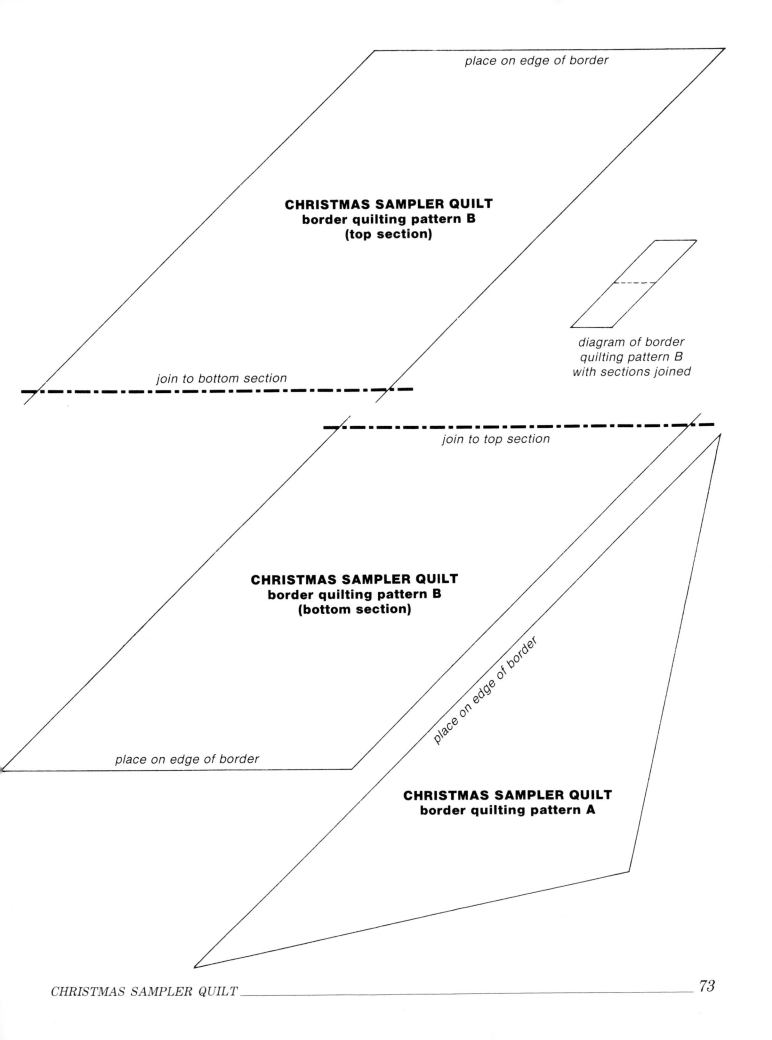

place on edge of border

CHRISTMAS SAMPLER QUILT
border quilting pattern B
(top section)

*diagram of border
quilting pattern B
with sections joined*

join to bottom section

join to top section

CHRISTMAS SAMPLER QUILT
border quilting pattern B
(bottom section)

place on edge of border

place on edge of border

CHRISTMAS SAMPLER QUILT
border quilting pattern A

(color photo, page 83)

4 Wedding Sampler Quilt

For this quilt, I wanted a soft, romantic look. I searched through my scrap boxes until I found a piece of chintz in shades of rose, soft green and gray—and that set my color scheme.

I looked for other fabrics in those colors, and finally settled on 18 different prints and solids. (That doesn't include the extra scraps I used to piece the Double Wedding Ring blocks.)

The big center medallion is surrounded by 14 blocks, some of which are repeated. Framing the medallion and blocks is sashing in a soft green print. The outside border is a dark print, and the edge is bound in a dark rose print.

The finished quilt is 91x109".

Materials

(Yardage is for fabric 45" wide.)

2¾ yd. dark print, for border
2½ yd. soft green print, for sashing
2 yd. off-white solid, for center medallion panel and piecing
1 yd. dark rose print, for bias binding
¼ yd. each of 6 assorted rose fabrics
¼ yd. each of 4 assorted green fabrics
¼ yd. each of 2 gray-and-rose prints (one light, one dark)
¼ yd. dark green, for leaves
Scraps of other fabrics in blending colors (optional)
7½ yd. print or solid, for backing, if you plan to assemble the whole top before quilting (*or* 10 yd. if you plan to quilt in sections)
1 pkg. dark green double-fold bias tape (3 yd.), for vine on center panel
Thread for piecing in white or blending color
Thread for appliqué in matching colors
Quilting thread in off-white or colors
Polyester batting: 1 pkg. 90x108", if you plan to assemble the whole top before quilting (*or* 1 pkg. 90x108" and ½ pkg. 72x90", if you plan to quilt in sections)
2 sheets of poster board (each cut to 16½x25½")

Prepare fabric

Prewash all the fabric if you plan to wash the finished quilt. Then cut off sections which will be used later for borders and bias binding.

From the print border fabric, cut 36" along the length to use for border pieces.

From the dark rose fabric, cut a 34" square for bias binding.

Set aside these sections and use remaining fabric to make the blocks.

Make medallion and blocks

Directions suggest the number of light, medium and dark colors needed for each block. You can use prints or solids, or a mix. When there is more than one fabric in a color group, it helps to number them—light color #1, light color #2, etc.

My list is only a guide. In some combinations, you'll find that a certain fabric seems to be a light color; in other combinations, it seems to be a medium color. Use your own judgment in putting the fabrics together.

For tips on making templates, piecing blocks and doing appliqué, see Chapter 1.

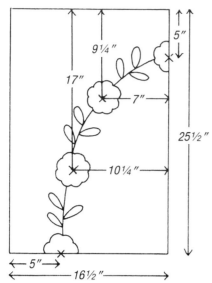

Fig. 1 *Template 1 for one-quarter of medallion*

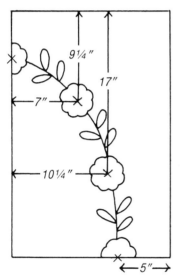

Fig. 2 *Template 2 for one-quarter of medallion*

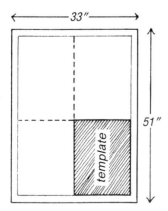

Fig. 3 *Using large template to mark center of medallion panel*

FLOWER WREATH

Let's do this center medallion first. It looks impressive, but it's easier than you might suspect.

The panel has 12 flowers appliquéd along an oval wreath of green bias tape. Each flower has three fabrics, and I repeated each combination twice, placing matching flowers opposite each other around the oval (see color photo, page 83).

Before you begin, read *Picture Appliqués*, page 8.

Make templates

Trace patterns for petals A and B, flower center and leaf, page 88, and make templates. You'll use petal A and the leaf to draft a picture template for the medallion.

Use one sheet of 16½x25½" poster board to draw Template 1 (Fig. 1). This is one-quarter of the medallion. From the top, measure 5" down the right edge, and mark an X. Center template for petal A over the X and trace half the flower.

Next, measure 7" across the top (from the right), then 9¼" down, and mark another X. Center petal A on the X and trace.

Measure 10¼" across the top (from the right), then 17" down, and mark an X. Center petal A on the X and trace.

Along the bottom, measure 5" from the left side, and mark an X. Center petal A on the X and trace half the flower.

With a pencil, draw a curved line joining the flowers. Use the leaf template and trace three leaves in each space between the flowers. When you are pleased with the diagram, go over the flowers, leaves and oval with a black pen.

Now you need to make Template 2—the same design in reverse (Fig. 2). Instead of measuring the spaces again, you can place tracing paper over Template 1 and trace your design. Then turn the tracing paper over (to reverse the design) and place it on top of the poster board for Template 2. Slip carbon paper between the layers and trace pattern onto the poster board.

Cut fabric for medallion

To mark the center panel, which is 33x51", use one of the large templates. Place the template on the wrong side of the off-white solid, keeping edges on the straight grain (Fig. 3). Trace two sides (outside lines of panel only), then move template to the next position for tracing. Keep shifting template until you have marked the full panel. Cut out fabric panel, adding ¼" to ½" seam allowances.

Keep the fabric wrong side up. Place Template 2, face down, on the fabric so that the design curves toward the center of the panel. Tape template in place. Turn fabric right side up, so you can see the template design through the fabric. Lightly trace the design onto the fabric with a hard No. 5H or 6H pencil.

Repeat step, positioning and tracing both templates to complete the oval. Now you'll know where the appliqués belong.

Do not cut templates apart. Save them for tracing the quilting designs later.

For each flower, you need three fabrics. Choose four different combinations, using dark fabrics for the large A petals.

Place templates on the right side of the fabric and trace. Cut out fabric, adding ¼" seam allowances:

    12 A petals of dark colors
      (2 each of 6 fabrics)
    12 B petals of lighter colors
      (2 each of 6 fabrics)

To cut and form the flower centers and leaves, follow directions for *Making perfect circles*, page 7. You will need:

    12 flower centers (2 each of
      6 fabrics)
    36 leaves of dark green

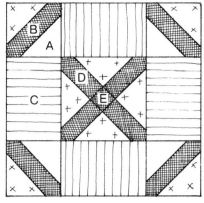

Fig. 4 *MAIDEN'S DELIGHT*
(color photo, page 49)

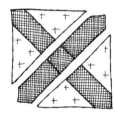

Fig. 5 *Piecing center square*

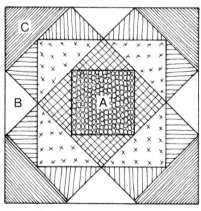

Fig. 6 *GENTLEMAN'S FANCY*
(color photo, page 84)

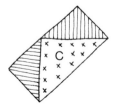

Fig. 7 *Piecing rectangle*

Position flowers

Stay-stitch appliqué pieces (optional) and slash seam allowances into V points and inside curves. Turn seam allowances, baste and press.

Position A petals on off-white panel, using your pencil outlines as a guide. Pin in place.

Lay green bias tape over curved lines between flowers. Cut lengths to fit and tuck ends under flowers. Baste bias in place so it won't shift.

Center a B petal on each A petal and pin. Add a flower center to each unit and pin.

Sew appliqués, beginning with the bottom layers. Use matching thread and the appliqué stitch (page 8).

Position leaves between flowers and sew in place.

Now sit back and admire your work before you go on to make the blocks.

MAIDEN'S DELIGHT

This handsome block had to be a part of the Wedding quilt, if only because of its name. The design is simple. Choose four fabrics—one light color, one medium and one dark, plus an off-white solid.

Make templates

Trace patterns A-E, page 89, and make templates.

Cut fabric

Place templates on the wrong side of the fabric and trace. Cut out, adding ¼" to ½" seam allowances:

    8 A triangles of light color
    4 A triangles of off-white solid
    4 B shapes of dark color
    4 C rectangles of medium color
    4 D shapes of dark color
    1 E square of dark color

Assemble

Lay pieces, face up, to form the block in Fig. 4.

Work with each corner. Pin-baste and stitch a light A triangle to one side of the B. Trim seam and finger-press to the darker side. Add an off-white A triangle to the opposite side of the B.

Begin the center square by piecing three diagonal rows (Fig. 5). Then join the rows.

Stitch the pieced squares and the C rectangles together to form three horizontal rows. Join the rows to complete the block.

GENTLEMAN'S FANCY

Here's another traditional block with an appropriate name. Choose six fabrics—one light color, three medium and one dark, plus off-white solid.

Make templates

Trace patterns A-C, page 90, and make templates.

Cut fabric

Place templates on wrong side of fabric and trace. Cut out, adding ¼" to ½" seam allowances:

    1 A square of medium color #1
    4 B triangles of off-white solid
    4 B triangles of medium color #2
    8 B triangles of medium color #3
    4 C triangles of light color
    4 C triangles of dark color

Assemble

Lay pieces, face up, to form the block in Fig. 6. You'll see that it's best to piece diagonal rows, then stitch the rows together.

First stitch a medium color #3 B triangle to each short edge of the light color C triangles (Fig. 7), making four rectangles.

Then work with the center

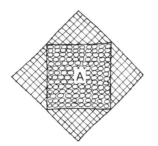

Fig. 8 *Piecing center square*

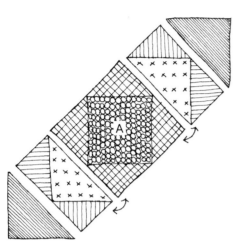

Fig. 9 *Piecing middle row*

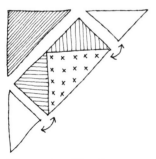

Fig. 10 *Piecing corner*

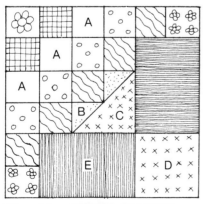

Fig. 11 **STEPS TO THE ALTAR**
(color photo, page 84)

square unit, adding a medium color #2 B triangle to each side of the A square (Fig. 8).

Complete the middle row (Fig. 9) by stitching a pieced rectangle to opposite sides of the center square. Add a dark C triangle to each end.

To form each of the two corner triangles (Fig. 10), first add an off-white B triangle to each end of the pieced rectangle. Complete by adding a dark C triangle.

Stitch the three diagonal rows together to make the block.

STEPS TO THE ALTAR

Diagonal rows of squares form the steps, and you'll find two of these blocks on the quilt, directly below the center medallion.

The arrangement of pattern pieces for one block is reversed, in order to form an interesting design when the blocks are placed side by side.

I chose nine fabrics—four light colors, four medium and one dark. Six of those fabrics were for the A squares (the steps). To use fewer fabrics, you could alternate just two colors for the diagonal rows of A squares.

Make templates
Trace patterns A-E, pages 92-93, and make templates.

Cut fabric
To help you keep track of the A squares, the list below follows the arrangement of A squares across the top of the block (left to right).

Place templates on the wrong side of the fabric. For each block, trace and cut out, adding ¼" to ½" seam allowances:

1 A square of light color #1
2 A squares of medium color #1
3 A squares of light color #2
4 A squares of light color #3

5 A squares of medium color #2
2 A squares of medium color #3
2 B triangles of medium color #4
1 C triangle of light color #4
1 D square of light color #4
2 E rectangles of dark color

Assemble
Lay all pieces, face up, to form the block in Fig. 11. Be sure A squares of the same fabric form diagonal rows.

First join the six A squares across the top to make a horizontal row.

Now work with the center section. Stitch the two B triangles to the A square (Fig. 12). Add this unit to the C triangle to form a large square.

Join A squares to form units (Fig. 13). Then stitch the units together, adding the large center square and the E rectangle to form a horizontal row.

To make the bottom row, first join the two vertical A squares. Stitch this unit to the E rectangle, then add the D square.

Stitch the three horizontal rows together to complete the block.

Be sure to reverse the line-up of fabric pieces when you make the second block.

HEART AND HOME

This is log cabin piecing with a heart appliqué in the center square. There are four of these blocks in the quilt, one at each corner, and you can piece them all in the same color sequence. You'll position the dark sides later when you add the hearts.

Choose nine fabrics for the piecing—four light (or medium) colors and four dark, plus off-white solid. Use a rose color for the hearts.

Make templates
Trace patterns for A and heart appliqué, page 91, and make templates. Then draft a template for the framing strips.

Fig. 12 *Forming the center square*

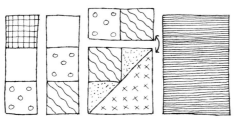

Fig. 13 *Joining pieces to form center row*

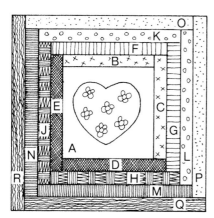

Fig. 14 **HEART AND HOME** (color photo, page 84)

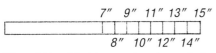

Fig. 15 *Making ruler template*

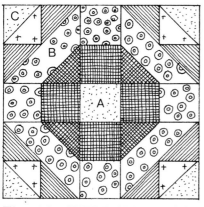

Fig. 16 **WEDDING RINGS** (color photo, page 84)

It's easy, and one strip will do it. On poster board or plastic, measure a rectangular strip 1″ wide and 15″ long. On the strip, measure up 7″ and mark a line across the template (Fig. 15). Add additional marks for 8″, 9″, 10″, 11″, 12″, 13″ and 14″. You have a ruler template.

Cut fabric

Place templates on the wrong side of the fabric and trace, using ruler template to mark the 1″-wide strips. When you cut out fabric, add ¼″ to ½″ seam allowances, and label each piece. For each block, you need:

    1 A square of off-white
    1 B (1x7″) of light color #1
    1 C (1x8″) of light color #1
    1 D (1x8″) of dark color #1
    1 E (1x9″) of dark color #1
    1 F (1x9″) of light color #2
    1 G (1x10″) of light color #2
    1 H (1x10″) of dark color #2
    1 J (1x11″) of dark color #2
    1 K (1x11″) of light color #3
    1 L (1x12″) of light color #3
    1 M (1x12″) of dark color #3
    1 N (1x13″) of dark color #3
    1 O (1x13″) of light color #4
    1 P (1x14″) of light color #4
    1 Q (1x14″) of dark color #4
    1 R (1x15″) of dark color #4

Assemble

Lay pieces, face up, to form the block in Fig. 14. Light color strips are at top and right of center square A. Dark colors are at bottom and left of A.

Add strips to square, beginning at the top with B. Work clockwise, adding the C strip, then the D strip, etc.

Piece all four blocks in this manner.

Add hearts

Place heart template on the right side of the rose fabric and trace four times. Cut out, adding ¼″ seam allowances.

Stay-stitch hearts (optional) and slash seam allowances into V points. Turn seam allowances, baste and press.

Lay the four pieced blocks in

front of you to form a large square, with the dark sides of each block on the outer edges of the large square. Position a heart appliqué in the center of each block, with the top of each heart along the top of the A square. Attach the hearts with matching thread and the appliqué stitch (page 8). Do not join the squares.

WEDDING RINGS

The large ring design (a rose print on my sampler) has a smaller ring inside. Make two Wedding Rings blocks, and you'll have one for each side of the quilt. Choose five fabrics— one light color, two medium and two dark.

Make templates

Trace patterns A-C, page 93, and make templates.

Cut fabric

Place templates on the wrong side of the fabric. For each block, trace and cut out, adding ¼″ to ½″ seam allowances:

    1 A square of medium
        color #1
    4 A squares of dark
        color #1
    4 A squares of medium
        color #2
    4 B shapes of medium
        color #2
    8 C triangles of dark
        color #2
    4 C triangles of light color
    4 C triangles of medium
        color #1
    4 C triangles of dark
        color #1

Assemble

Lay all pieces, face up, to form the block in Fig. 16. Look closely, and see how you can begin piecing the corner squares.

Stitch each light color C triangle to a medium color #1 C triangle to make small squares

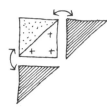

Fig. 17 *Piecing large corner triangle*

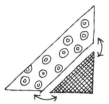

Fig. 18 *Piecing second large triangle*

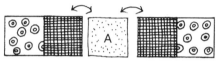

Fig. 19 *Forming center row*

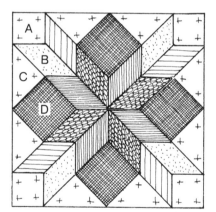

Fig. 20 **LOVE-IN-A-MIST**
(color photo, page 84)

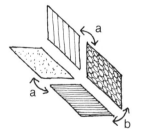

Fig. 21 *Joining B shapes*

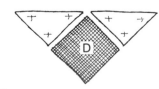

Fig. 22 *Forming large triangle*

(Fig. 17). Add two dark color #2 C triangles to adjacent sides of each square to make four large triangles.

Next add a dark color #1 C triangle to the short side of each B shape to make four larger triangles (Fig. 18).

Join two large triangle units to form each corner square.

To make four rectangles, stitch a medium color #1 A square to each dark color #1 A square.

Form a center horizontal row by stitching a rectangle to opposite sides of the center square (Fig. 19). Join other pieced units to make top and bottom horizontal rows. Finally, stitch the three rows together to complete the block.

I did mention that there should be two of these blocks, didn't I?

LOVE-IN-A-MIST

The B shapes in this block are rhomboids (adjacent sides are different lengths). Piece them like diamonds, but be sure to reverse the template as indicated when you mark the fabric.

Make a pair of these blocks so you'll have one for each side of the center medallion. Choose six fabrics—one light color, three medium and two dark.

Make templates
Trace patterns A-D, page 94, and make templates.

Cut fabric
Place templates on the wrong side of the fabric. For each block, trace and cut out, adding ¼" to ½" seam allowances:
   4 A squares of light color
   4 B shapes of medium color #1
   4 B shapes of dark color #1
   4 B shapes (reversed) of medium color #2

4 B shapes (reversed) of medium color #3
8 C triangles of light color
4 D squares of dark color #2

Assemble
Lay all pieces, face up, to form the block in Fig. 20. Stitch adjacent B shapes together in pairs along the short edges (Fig. 21, a).

Join the units (Fig. 2I, b). If you use a machine, stitch the units together only from end point to end point; do not stitch into seam allowances. (See *Piecing diamonds,* page 4.)

Join the pieced units at the center of the block—like a star.

Form four large side triangles by stitching two C triangles to each D square (Fig. 22). Piece in these large side triangles and the corner A squares to complete the design.

Now that you've conquered this block, you can easily make another one.

DOUBLE WEDDING RING

The Double Wedding Ring, with its intricate piecing, is one of the most admired quilt patterns. After you make two of these blocks for your sampler, you can decide whether you'd like to piece a whole quilt of the rings.

I hope you've been saving all your scraps. Choose two colors for the A pieces, placing color #1 at one end of each curve, and color #2 at the other end of each curve. For the B and C pieces in between, use any assortment of colors you like.

The large background pieces are off-white solid to emphasize the colorful rings.

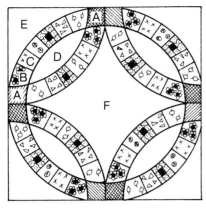

Fig. 23 **DOUBLE WEDDING RING**

(color photo, page 84)

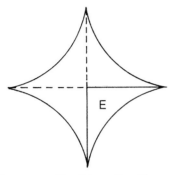

Fig. 24 *Drafting the F template*

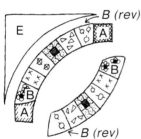

Fig. 25 *Assembling ring pieces for one unit*

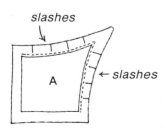

slashes

← slashes

Fig. 26 *Slashing concave curves*

Make templates

Trace patterns A-E, page 95, and make templates.

Use the E template to draft the large center F piece. Trace around the E piece four times, butting the straight edges together (Fig. 24).

Cut fabric

Place templates on the wrong side of the fabric. For each block, trace and cut out, adding ¼" to ½" seam allowances:

4 A pieces of color #1
4 A pieces of color #2
8 B pieces of assorted colors
8 B (reversed) pieces of assorted colors
32 C pieces of assorted colors
4 D pieces of off-white solid
4 E pieces of off-white solid
1 F piece of off-white solid

Assemble

Begin by arranging ring pieces to form a quarter of the block (Fig. 25). The longer curve fits against an E piece, and it has an A at each end. Use color #l for the A at the left end, and color #2 for the A at the right end. Place a B next to the A at left, and a B (reversed) next to the A at the right. Arrange the four C pieces in between.

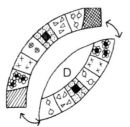

Fig. 27 *Joining curved pieces*

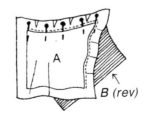

Fig. 28 *Adding ring units to the D piece*

For the shorter curve, place a B at the right end, and a B (reversed) at the left end, with four C pieces in between.

You'll notice that each A piece has two concave (inside) curves, and you must slash these before stitching them to the B pieces. (You may want to stay-stitch the curves just outside the pencil lines first.) Slash along the curves almost to the pencil lines (Fig. 26).

Work with the longer curve. Pin-baste an A to a B (reversed), placing pins perpendicular to the curved line (Fig. 27). Then turn the fabric over and stitch on the B side—along the convex curve. It seems to go together easier this way.

Repeat, joining an A to a B at the opposite end of the curve. Then complete the ring unit by stitching the A/B units and the C pieces together.

Complete the shorter ring unit by stitching the B and C pieces together.

Next sew the shorter ring unit to the D piece (Fig. 28). Prepare the concave curve on the ring by stay-stitching (optional) and slashing almost to the pencil line. Pin-baste ring to the D (ring side up), then stitch (with D side up).

Before sewing the longer ring unit to the D, prepare the concave curve on the ring unit in the same manner. Pin-baste to D and stitch.

Follow the same steps to piece the three remaining ring segments.

Lay all the pieces, face up, to form the design in Fig. 23. Be sure the A colors are in the same position in each ring segment.

Prepare the concave curves on the F piece, then pin-baste and stitch to each ring segment. Add the E corner pieces in the same way to complete the block.

Pretty, isn't it? You'll need one more for the quilt. Would you like to make a whole quilt of Double Wedding Ring blocks?

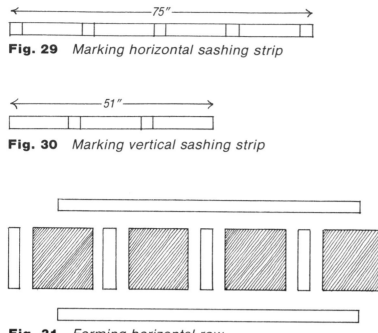

←——————————— 75″ ———————————→

Fig. 29 *Marking horizontal sashing strip*

←————— 51″ —————→

Fig. 30 *Marking vertical sashing strip*

Fig. 31 *Forming horizontal row*

Complete quilt top

Now that the central medallion and blocks are made, it's time to add the sashing and cut the border pieces.

Cut sashing

Draft two templates—one 3x15″ and one 3″ square. To mark the long horizontal sashing strips, use both templates and work along the lengthwise grain. On the wrong side of the fabric, first trace the 3″ square. Then butt the 3x15″ template against the square and trace it. Move and trace the two templates in this manner until you have a 3x75″ strip (Fig. 29). Mark 3 more strips in the same way, leaving room for seam allowances between them.

The pencil cross marks on each strip will line up with the corners of blocks when you assemble rows.

To mark the long vertical sashing strips, again use both templates, but begin with the 3x15″ piece. Then trace the 3″ square. Move and trace the two templates until you have a 3x51″ strip (Fig. 30). Mark 3

more strips in the same way, leaving room for seam allowances between them.

To mark the short sashing strips, use the 3x15″ template and trace 14 strips, leaving room for seam allowances.

Cut out all sashing strips, adding ¼″ to ½″ seam allowances.

Assemble sections

Lay the finished quilt blocks in position on the floor, forming a horizontal row at the top and bottom, and vertical rows at the sides. Place short sashing strips between the blocks. On the top and bottom rows only, also add a short strip at each end (Fig. 31).

Stitch blocks and sashing strips together to make the top and bottom rows. Then add a 3x75″ strip to the top and bottom of each row, matching pencil cross marks on the strips to corners of the blocks.

Stitch blocks and short sashing strips together to make the vertical rows. Add a 3x51″ strip to each side of the rows, matching pencil cross marks on the strips to corners of the blocks.

Cut border pieces

Make a template 7½″ wide and about 15″ long (you can slide the template along when marking fabric).

Place template on the wrong side of the border fabric and mark needed lengths. Cut out fabric, adding ¼″ to ½″ seam allowances:

2 strips, 7½x93″ each
2 strips, 7½x90″ each

Transfer lines for the outside edges of the quilt to the right side of each border piece by basting over your pencil lines.

Finish quilt

If you plan to join the top before quilting, see Quilting the whole top, page 149. Stitch a side row of blocks to each side of the center medallion. Add the top and bottom rows of blocks. Add the border pieces, first the sides and then the top and bottom. Also piece the backing fabric, following Fig. 32 as a guide.

If you plan to quilt in sections, see Quilting in sections, page 150. Work with the individual rows, center medallion and border pieces before stitching them together.

Mark quilting lines

Press finished top (whole or sections).

Mark lines or designs on the center medallion, the blocks and border as listed below. (See *Marking simple lines and shapes,* page 147, and *Marking special designs,* page 148.)

Center medallion—Please get out the large Templates 1 and 2 you made for the center panel. You can now add the quilting designs to the templates and then transfer them to the fabric.

First make special cut-out templates for the rose and the leaf, page 88. Trace the complete patterns, including inside

(continued on page 87)

Wedding Sampler Quilt

Gentleman's Fancy, page 77

Steps to the Altar, page 78

Heart and Home, page 78

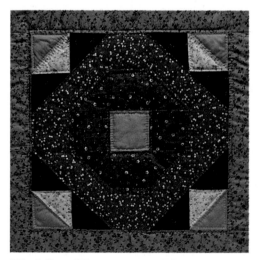

Wedding Rings, page 79

Love-in-a-Mist, page 80

Double Wedding Ring, page 80

Checkerboard and Schoolhouse Wall Hanging, page 137

Glittering Star Quilt, page 105

LET'S MAKE MORE PATCHWORK QUILTS

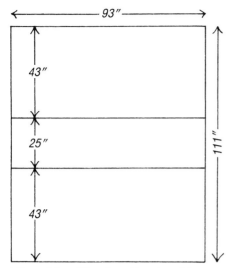

Fig. 32 *Piecing the backing (if you quilt the top as a whole)*

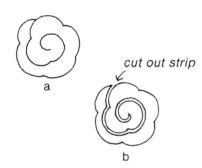

Fig. 33 *Making cut-out template*

Fig. 34 *Adding quilting designs to Template 1*

(continued from page 82)

design lines; then transfer them to poster board.

Cut out the rose shape (Fig. 33, a). To expose the inside quilting line, cut along the line. Then cut a second line about $1/16''$ away, and remove the narrow strip of poster board (b).

Repeat to make cut-out leaf template.

Position quilting templates on Template 1, using Fig. 34 as a guide. In the upper left corner, trace three roses in a curve, keeping them at least $1\frac{1}{4}''$ from the top and side. Add leaf outlines between roses and at each end, reversing the template as needed.

Add the center wreath. Measure $9''$ down the right edge and mark an X. Center template for rose over the X and trace half the flower.

Arrange and trace the rose template four more times; the edge of the last rose will be $4\frac{1}{2}''$ from the right edge.

Add leaf outlines between roses, reversing the template as needed.

Finally, go over lines with a black pen. Repeat steps to add quilting lines to Template 2 (reversing the design). Be sure to match the half roses and leaves where they come together.

With a hard pencil, transfer the quilting designs to fabric, just as you did the appliqué outlines.

Also mark diagonal lines to crisscross on the fabric background (or wait until layers are basted for quilting and use masking tape as a guide). Draw first line from corner to corner, then place additional lines $1\frac{3}{4}''$ apart (skipping the appliqués and quilting lines for roses and leaves).

Heart and Home corner blocks—Mark the hearts with crisscrossing diagonal lines, $3/4''$ apart.

Maiden's Delight—Mark diagonal lines to crisscross on the large C rectangles; draw the first line from corner to corner,

then add additional lines $3/4''$ apart.

Gentleman's Fancy—Mark diagonal lines on center square, following directions above. On each large C triangle, mark a smaller triangle $3/4''$ from seam lines.

Double Wedding Ring—Mark center of block with the rose quilting design, page 95.

Steps to the Altar—Mark the corner D square with the heart quilting design, page 92. Place heart on the diagonal, with top of heart toward center of block. Inside each large rectangle, mark two smaller rectangles, $3/4''$ apart.

Border—On my sampler, I quilted heart shapes all around the dark print border (although they don't show up in the photograph). Bottom tips of all hearts point to bottom of quilt.

Use your heart appliqué template from the Heart and Home block. Trace 13 hearts, evenly spaced, across the top and bottom border pieces. Trace 15 hearts, evenly spaced, along each side border piece. (If your marks won't show on the border fabric, you can wait until you're ready to quilt. At that time, cut a heart template from nonwoven interfacing, pin it in place and quilt around it. Then move the template to the next position for quilting.)

Quilting guides

Stack the layers, smoothing quilt top over backing and batting. Baste the layers together.

Before you begin stitching, see *Making quilting stitches,* page 148. Quilt blocks and sashing pieces, following guides under *Basic quilting,* page 147. Also quilt the lines and designs you have marked.

Finish edges

Make bias from the $34''$ square of dark rose print, and stitch bias to the quilt. Follow directions under *Using continuous bias,* page 151.

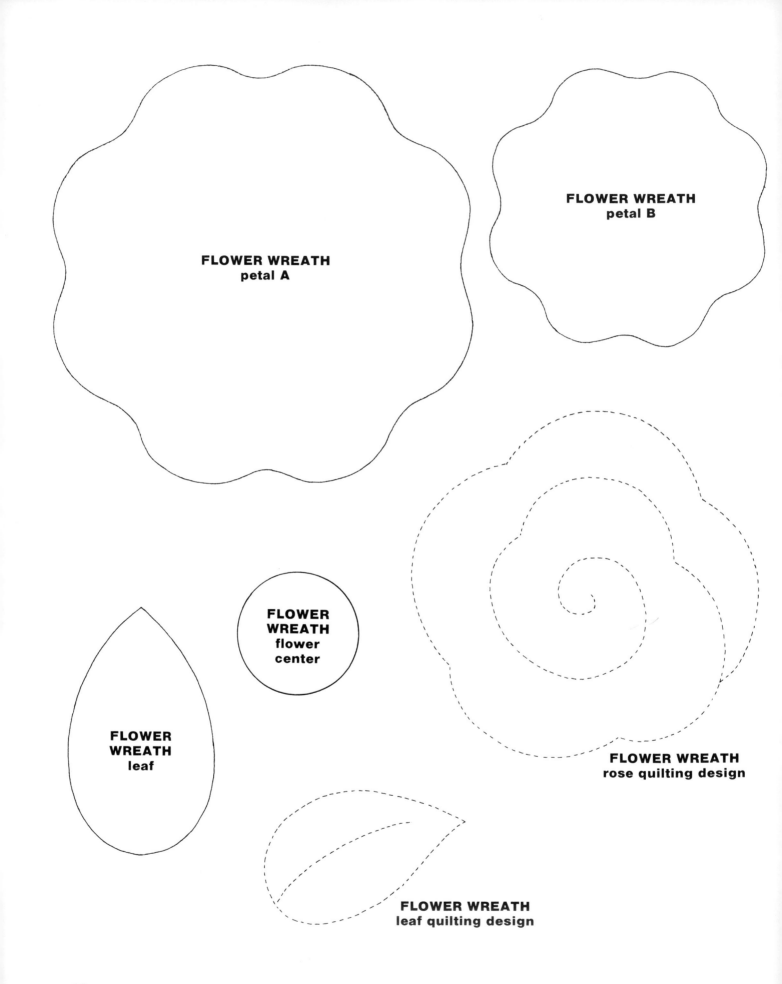

FLOWER WREATH
petal A

FLOWER WREATH
petal B

FLOWER
WREATH
flower
center

FLOWER
WREATH
leaf

FLOWER WREATH
rose quilting design

FLOWER WREATH
leaf quilting design

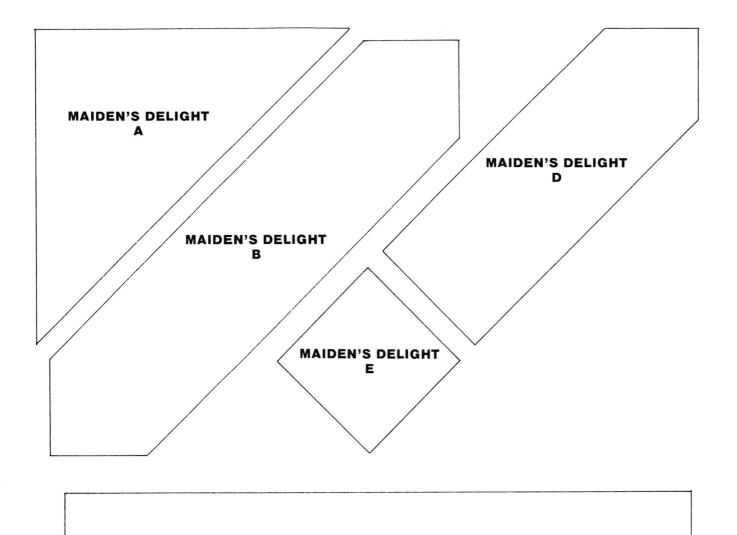

MAIDEN'S DELIGHT
A

MAIDEN'S DELIGHT
B

MAIDEN'S DELIGHT
D

MAIDEN'S DELIGHT
E

MAIDEN'S DELIGHT
C

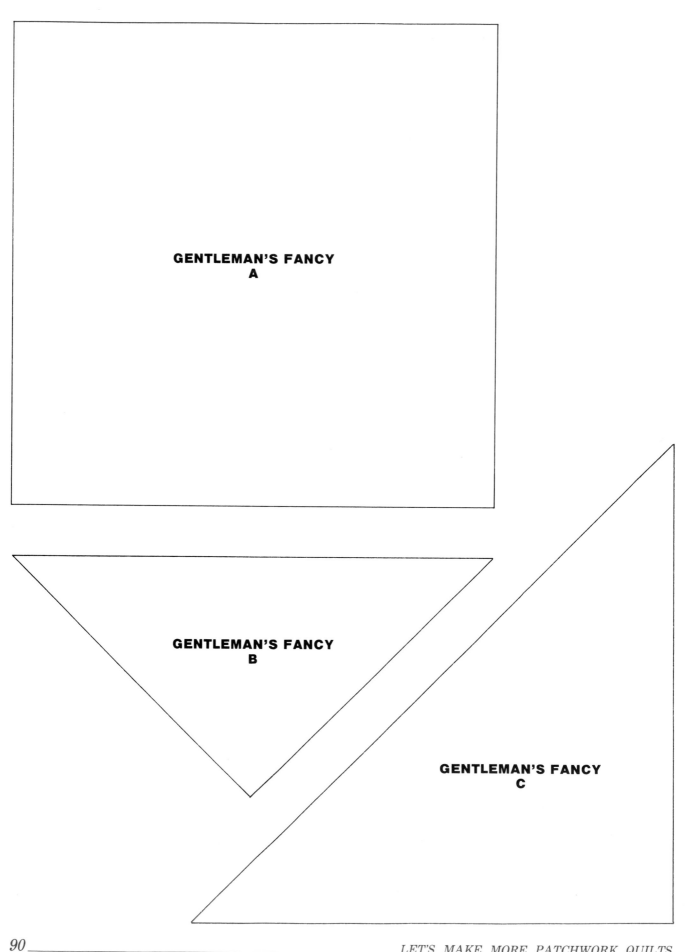

GENTLEMAN'S FANCY
A

GENTLEMAN'S FANCY
B

GENTLEMAN'S FANCY
C

heart appliqué

HEART AND HOME
A

STEPS TO THE ALTAR
D
(with heart quilting design)

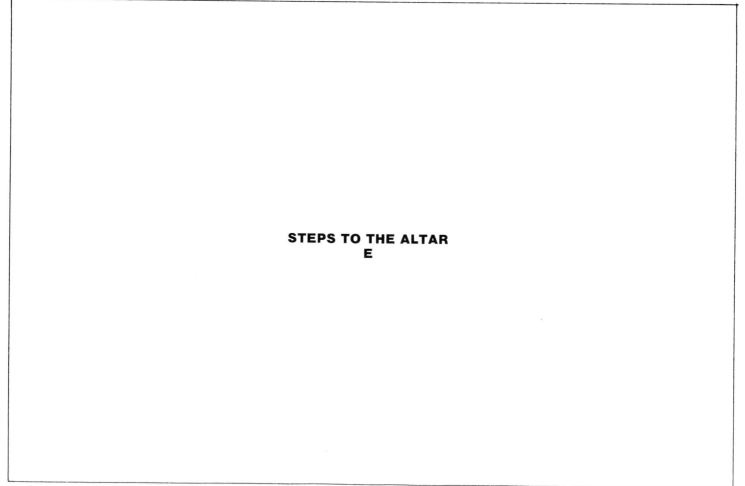

STEPS TO THE ALTAR
E

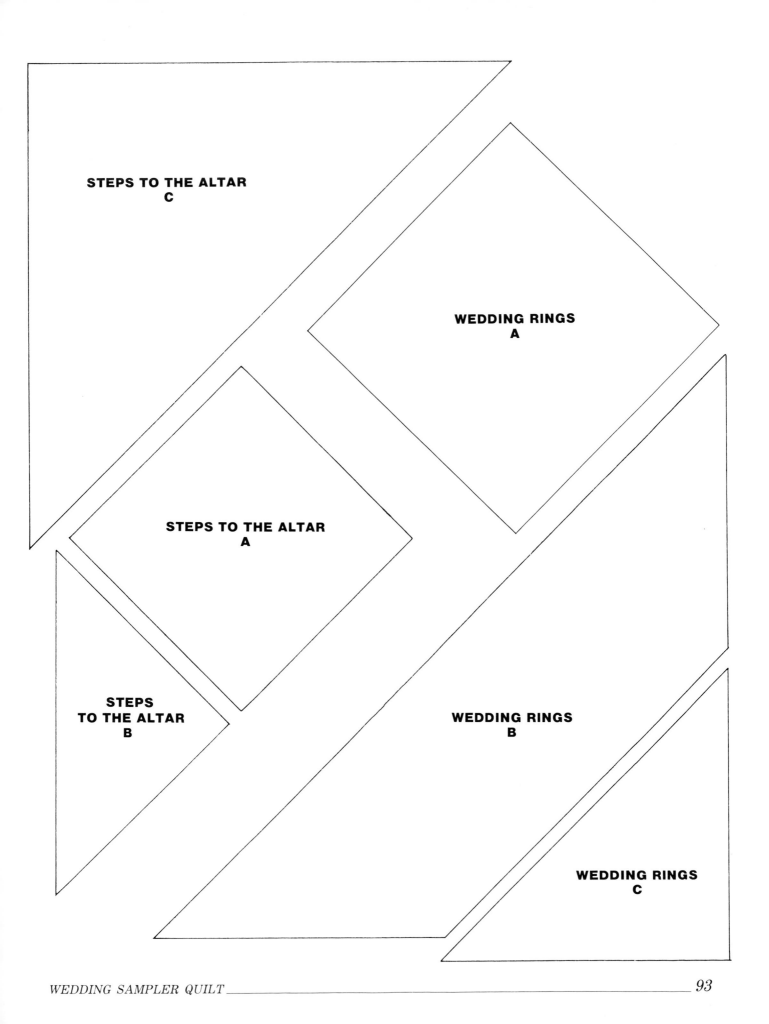

STEPS TO THE ALTAR
C

WEDDING RINGS
A

STEPS TO THE ALTAR
A

STEPS
TO THE ALTAR
B

WEDDING RINGS
B

WEDDING RINGS
C

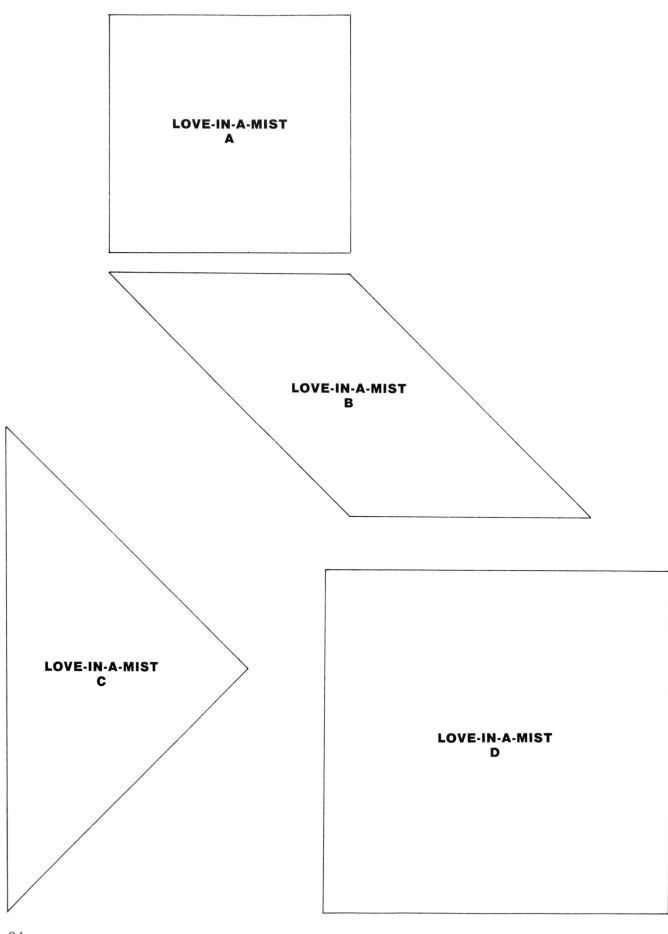

LOVE-IN-A-MIST
A

LOVE-IN-A-MIST
B

LOVE-IN-A-MIST
C

LOVE-IN-A-MIST
D

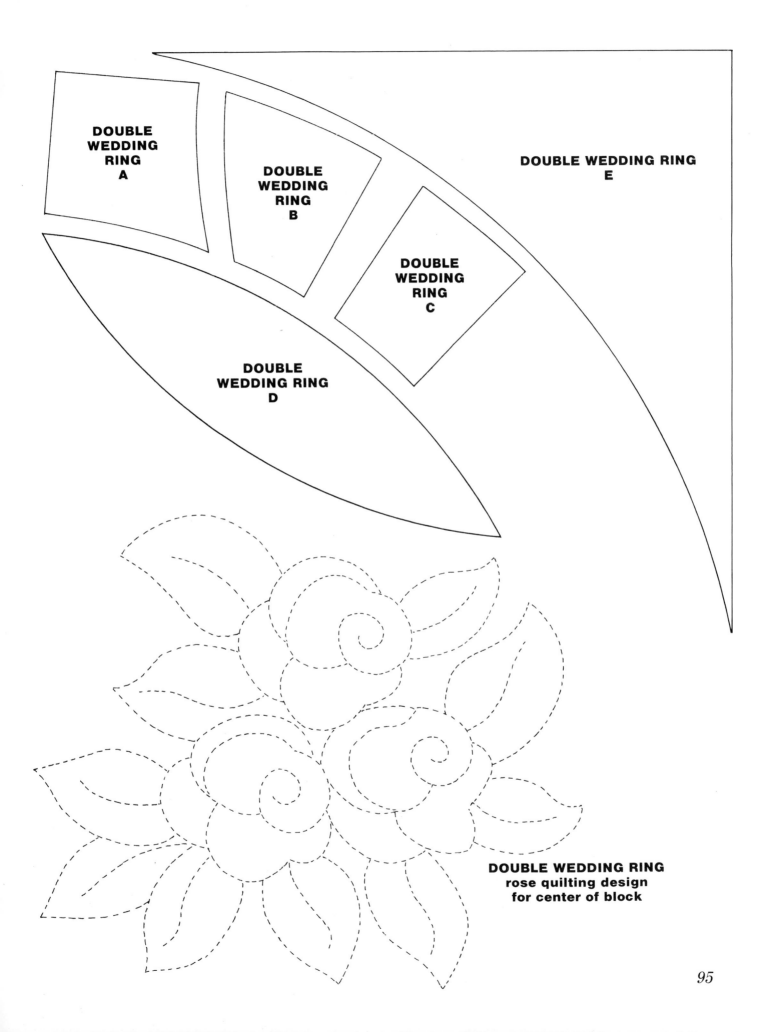

DOUBLE WEDDING RING A

DOUBLE WEDDING RING B

DOUBLE WEDDING RING C

DOUBLE WEDDING RING E

DOUBLE WEDDING RING D

DOUBLE WEDDING RING
rose quilting design
for center of block

95

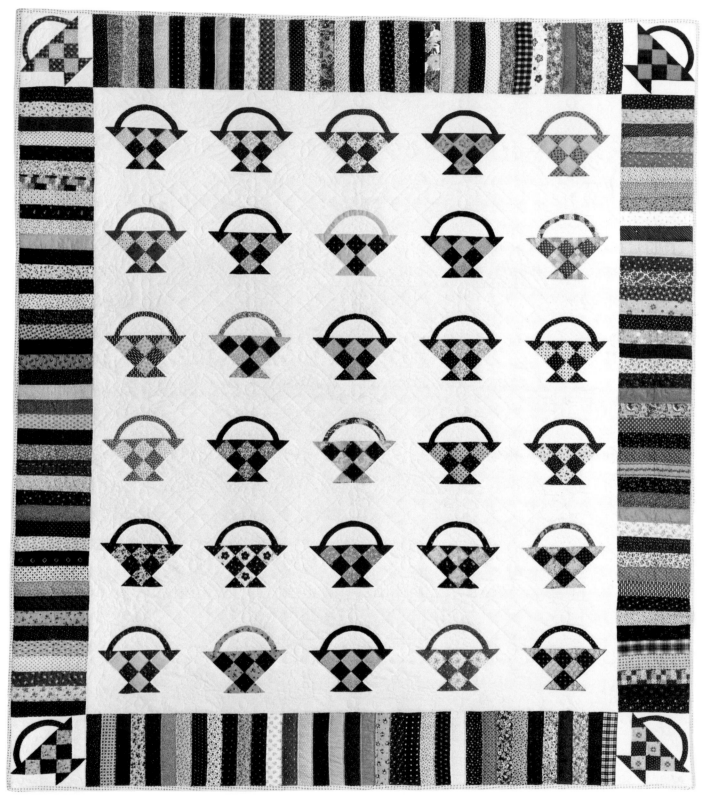

(color photo, page 47)

LET'S MAKE MORE PATCHWORK QUILTS

5 Scrap Basket Quilt

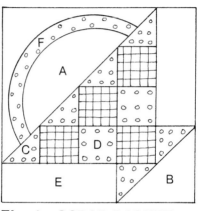

Fig. 1 *SCRAP BASKET*

Fabrics left over from other sewing projects are ideal for this quilt. I had enough scraps to make each basket in a different fabric combination, using 68 scraps (plus off-white) for the 34 baskets. I repeated these fabrics in the border, adding other strips to make a total of 154. A true scrap quilt!

You can use fewer fabrics, repeating them in several blocks, or you can make the whole quilt with just three fabrics—two colors and an off-white solid.

The quilt block requires two techniques—piecing for the basket and appliqué for the handle. Finished blocks are set between alternate blocks of off-white solid. These white blocks are later quilted in the basket pattern.

You can sew the whole quilt top together before quilting, or you can quilt in sections. You may want to read about these two methods of quilting in Chapter 12 before you begin.

The finished quilt is 90x104".

Materials
(Yardage is for fabric 45" wide.)

5 yd. off-white solid fabric
Many, many scraps of prints and/or solids, for baskets and border
8 yd. print or solid, for backing, if you plan to assemble the whole top before quilting (*or* 12 yd. if you plan to quilt in sections)
1 yd. print or solid, for bias binding
Thread for piecing in white or blending color
Thread for appliqué in matching colors
Quilting thread in white or colors
Polyester batting: 1 pkg. 90x108", if you plan to assemble the whole top before quilting (*or* 1 pkg. 90x108" and ½ pkg. 72x90", if you plan to quilt in sections)

If you prefer to use just two fabrics besides off-white, omit the scraps listed above and substitute: 4½ yd. of one print or solid, for basket pieces (including all handles) and border pieces, and 3¼ yd. of a contrasting print or solid, for remaining basket and border pieces. Also add 1 yd. extra of off-white solid to use for bias binding.

Prepare fabric

Prewash all the fabric if you plan to wash the finished quilt.

From the bias binding fabric, cut a 34" square. Set the square aside and use remaining section for the blocks.

Make blocks

For tips on making templates, piecing blocks and doing appliqué, see Chapter 1.

Make templates
Trace patterns A-F, pages 99-100, and make templates.

Cut fabric
For each basket block, use three fabrics—off-white solid and two colors (prints, solids or one of each). Label the colors #1 and #2 to help you in tracing templates.

Place templates on the wrong side of the fabric and trace. Cut out, adding ¼" to ½" seam allowances:
    1 A triangle of off-white solid
    1 B triangle of off-white solid
    6 C triangles of color #1
    2 D squares of color #1
    4 D squares of color #2
    2 E rectangles of off-white solid
Place handle template F on right side of color #1 and trace. Cut out, adding ¼" seam allowances.

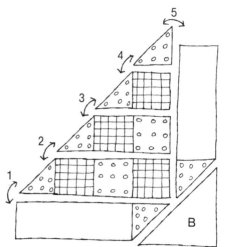

Fig. 2 *Piecing basket*

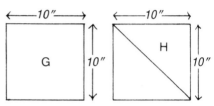

Fig. 3 *Drafting large templates*

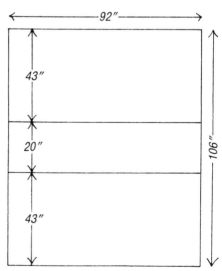

Fig. 4 *Piecing the backing (if you quilt the whole top)*

Fig. 5 *Guide for cutting backing (if you quilt in sections)*

Assemble

Set handle piece aside. Lay other pieces, face up, to form the block in Fig. 1.

Work on the basket section, first forming rows (Fig. 2). Pin-baste and stitch pieces together, matching pencil lines and end points. Trim each seam and finger-press to the darker side.

Stitch rows together, following numbers on Fig. 2. Add the B triangle last.

For the handle appliqué, stay-stitch the curved seams (optional) and slash seam allowance along the inside curve. Turn seam allowances on curves, baste and press.

Center handle on the A triangle (see Fig. 1). Raw edges at ends of handle will be even with raw edge of triangle. Sew handle along the curves with matching thread and the appliqué stitch (page 8).

Join the two large triangle units to complete the block. There you are—only 33 more basket blocks to assemble.

Complete quilt top

After the basket blocks are pieced and appliquéd, you are ready to put them into rows and make the quilt borders.

Cut alternate blocks

You'll have to draft two large templates—G and H (Fig. 3). Square G has 10" sides. Triangle H is half of a G square. To draw it, divide the square with a diagonal line.

Also trace pattern J, page 101, and make a template.

Place templates on the wrong side of the off-white solid and trace. Cut out fabric, adding ¼" to ½" seam allowances:
  20 G squares
  18 H triangles
  4 J triangles

Assemble rows

Lay your basket blocks and off-white alternate blocks on the floor, following Fig. 6. The blocks form diagonal rows, with off-white H triangles all around the edges and a J triangle at each corner.

Stitch blocks and triangles together to form diagonal rows.

Cut border pieces

Trace pattern for border strip, page 103, and make a template.

Place template on the wrong side of the fabric and trace. Cut out, adding ¼" to ½" seam allowances.

You'll need 154 border strips in all. I know that's a lot of cutting, but if you're using scraps, it's fun to play with the colors.

Assemble borders

Arrange fabric pieces to form each border section. There are 42 strips on each side and 35 strips on both top and bottom.

Stitch strips together to form the four sections. Then stitch a basket block to each end of the top and bottom sections.

The outside edges of the quilt are marked on the wrong side of each border section. To transfer these guidelines to the right side, baste over the pencil lines.

Finish quilt

If you plan to join the whole top before quilting, see Quilting the whole top, page 149. Stitch the diagonal rows together, being careful to match the corner points. Add each side border section, then add the top and bottom border sections. Also piece the backing fabric, following Fig. 4.

If you plan to quilt in sections, see Quilting in sections, page 150. Join rows to make four units, as shown in Fig. 6.

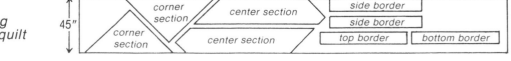

Each corner section has three rows. Each center section has two rows. Cut backing strips as you need them, using Fig. 5 as a guide. Quilt each section before joining it to another quilted section.

Mark quilting lines

Press the finished top (whole or sections).

Trace quilting designs for H and J, page 101. Trace quilting design for G, pages 102-103, joining the two sections on broken lines.

Transfer designs to your G, H and J templates, then trace them onto the matching off-white pieces of your quilt top. (See *Marking special designs*, page 148.) Use the G template under the pieced blocks to mark a petal shape in each corner and a flower under each basket handle.

Quilting guides

Stack the layers. Smooth quilt top over backing and batting. Baste the layers together.

Before you begin stitching, see *Making quilting stitches*, page 148.

Quilt blocks, following general guides under *Basic quilting*, page 147. Additional suggestions are below.

On each pieced basket, quilt inside the four squares of color #2 only. Quilt around basket and handle. Also quilt the petal shapes and the flower design you marked.

On the off-white blocks, quilt design lines you marked.

Finish edges

Make bias from the 34″ square of fabric you saved, and stitch the bias to the quilt. Follow directions under *Using continuous bias*, page 151.

**SCRAP BASKET
D**

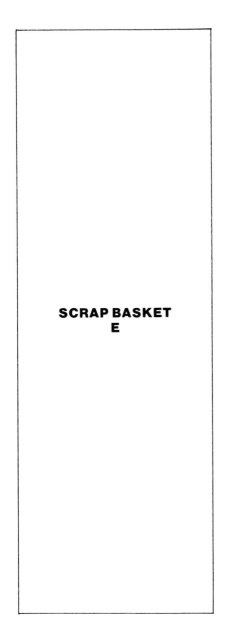

**SCRAP BASKET
E**

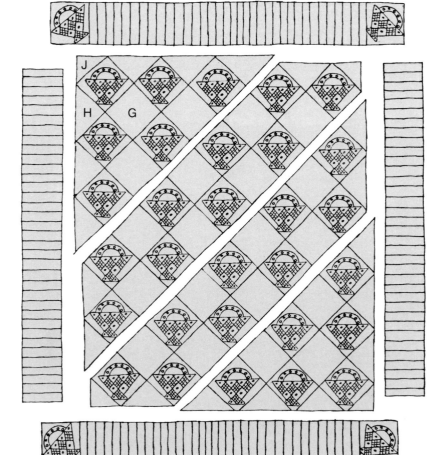

Fig. 6 *General layout for Scrap Basket quilt, showing units for quilting in sections*

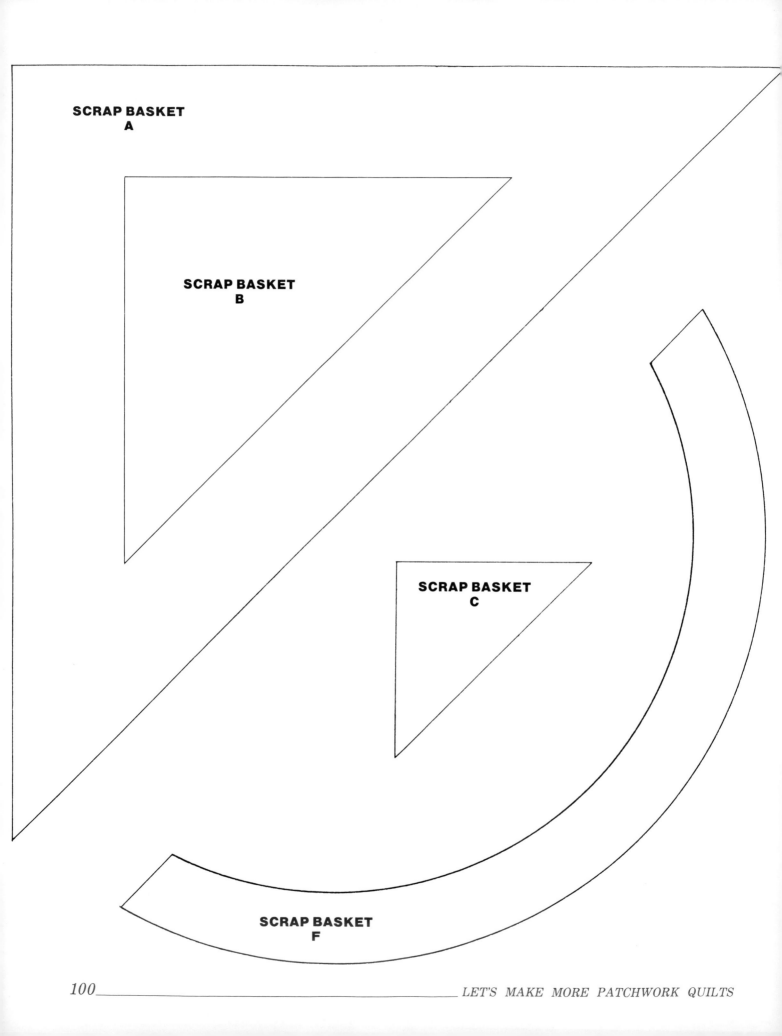

SCRAP BASKET
A

SCRAP BASKET
B

SCRAP BASKET
C

SCRAP BASKET
F

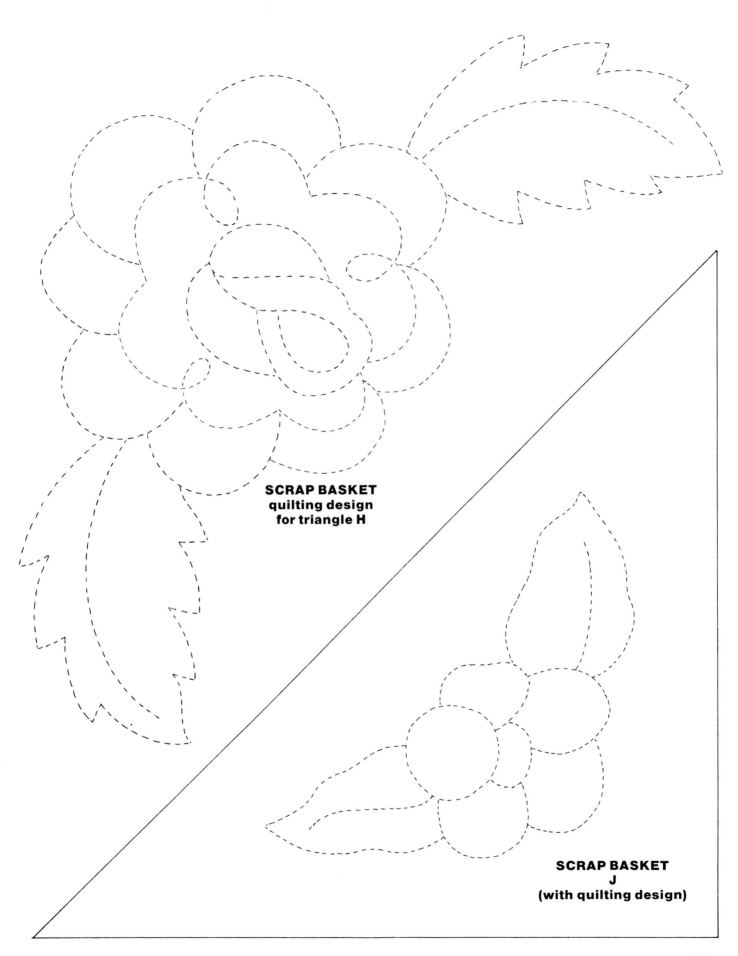

SCRAP BASKET
quilting design
for triangle H

SCRAP BASKET
J
(with quilting design)

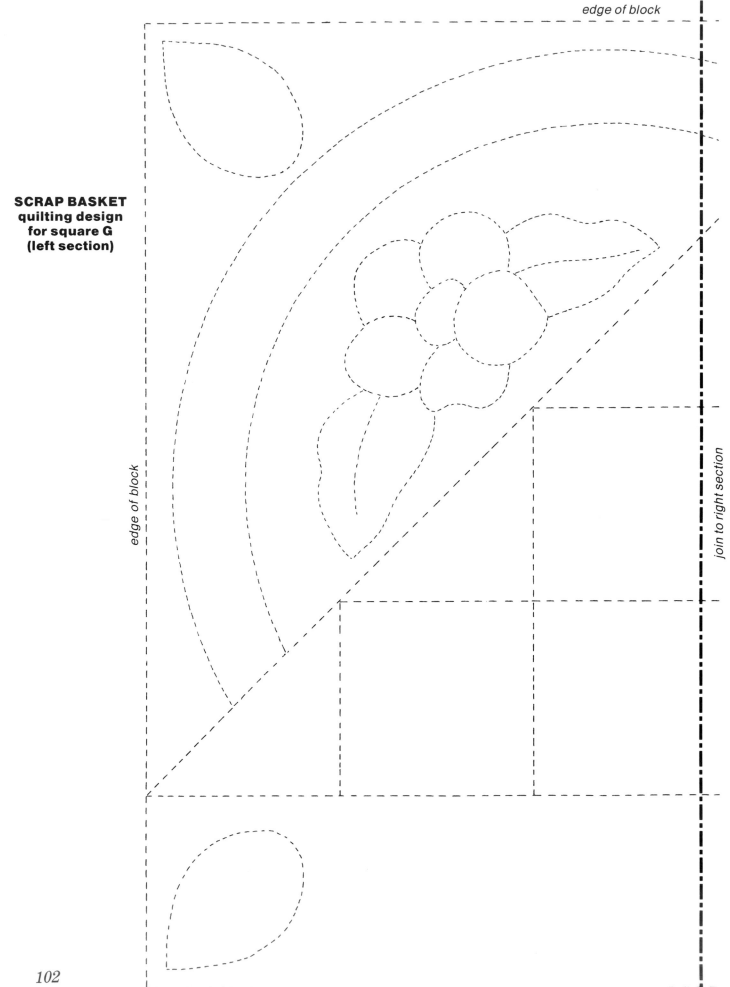

SCRAP BASKET
quilting design
for square G
(left section)

edge of block

edge of block

edge of block

join to right section

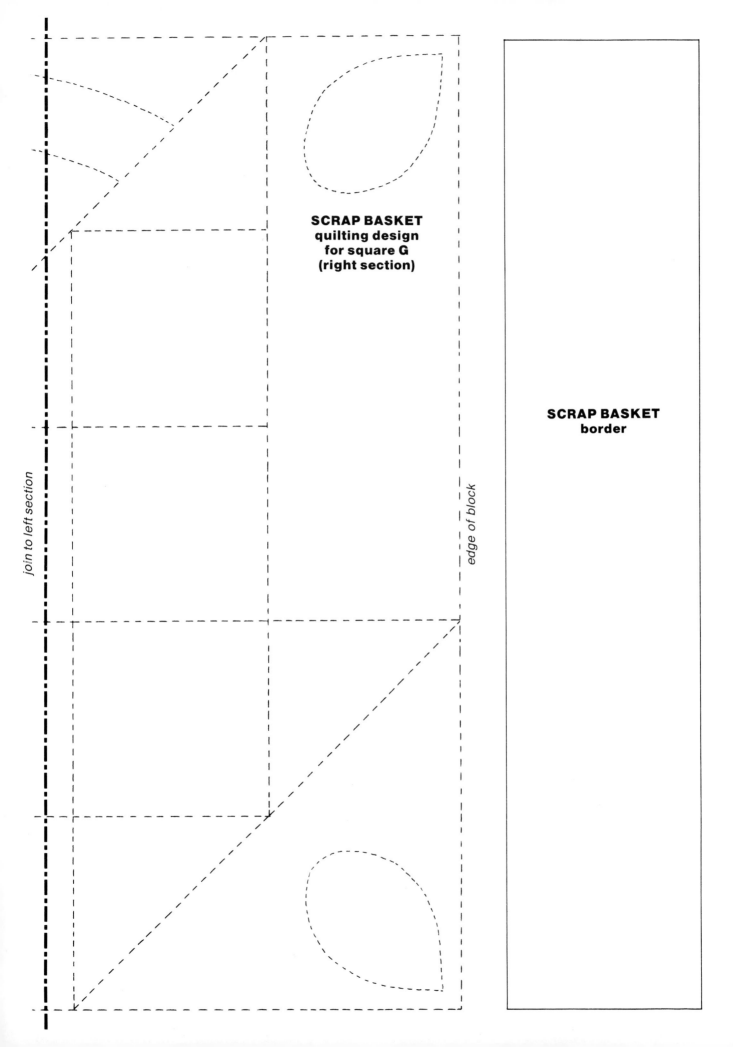

SCRAP BASKET
quilting design
for square G
(right section)

join to left section

edge of block

SCRAP BASKET
border

(color photo, page 86)

6 Glittering Star Quilt

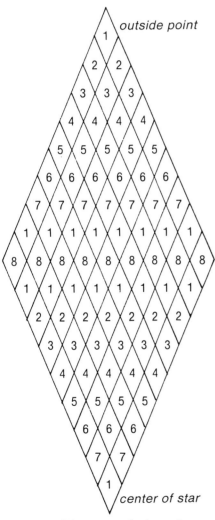

outside point

center of star

Fig. 1 *Diagram of pieced diamond (star point)*

Almost every quilter, I've discovered, harbors a desire to make a giant star quilt like this one. The main Glittering Star design has several other names, including Lone Star and Star of Bethlehem.

I've added an extra panel with two Eight-Pointed Star blocks at the top to make the shape a rectangle. When you spread this quilt over a double bed, you'll see a small star on each pillow.

The finished quilt size is 89½x106½". For a wall hanging, you might prefer to make just the square shape, omitting the top panel.

This is one quilt top that you must piece and assemble completely before quilting. Then you will need to use a quilting frame or a hoop.

If you've already pieced an Eight-Pointed Star block like those at the top, you'll notice that Glittering Star is really nothing but an eight-pointed star divided into many small diamonds.

If you've never pieced a star, you can try one 15" block to see how you like it. Use the D, E and F patterns on page 109, and follow directions for *Piecing diamonds*, page 4. I'll bet you'll love it and will want to make the whole quilt.

Before we think about choosing fabric, let's decide on the colors. Should they be all solids? All prints? Shades of brown? Shades of blue? Take your choice. I chose primary colors (red, yellow and blue) in prints and solids. Then I added green, white and black prints that have the primary colors in them. The black background and red border strips create a dramatic look. All the quilting lines are hand-stitched in red.

To help you decide, trace Fig. 1 and use colored pencils to try your color sequence. When you are satisfied, make a list to match numbers with colors, like the one below. (This is the list for my sample quilt.)

1. Black print
2. Red print
3. Red solid
4. Yellow print
5. Blue print
6. Blue solid
7. Green print
8. White print

Next, choose a color for the background and outside border (I used black), as well as a color for the inside border strips (I used red).

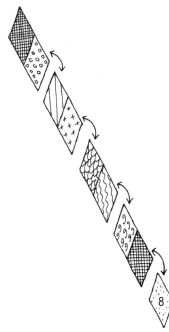

Fig. 2 *Forming a row*

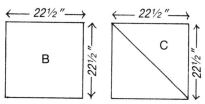

Fig. 3 *Drafting large templates*

Materials

(Yardage is for fabric 45" wide.)

4¾ yd. solid color, for background squares and triangles, and outside border (black on sample)

1¼ yd. print or solid for No. 1 diamonds

¾ yd. each of 7 other prints or solids, for all other diamonds

9 yd. solid, for inside border strips, bias edging and backing (red on sample)

Thread for piecing in blending color

Quilting thread in color of your choice (red on sample)

1 pkg. polyester batting, 90x108"

Prepare fabric

Prewash all fabric if you plan to wash the finished quilt. Then cut off sections which will be used later for making borders and bias binding.

From the background fabric, cut a section 22x100" for the outside border.

From inside border fabric, cut a section 15x95" for the border. Also cut a 36" square for bias binding.

Set these sections aside and use remaining lengths for piecing the quilt top.

Piece large star

For tips on making templates and general piecing, see Chapter 1.

The large star has eight star points (large diamonds), and each star point is divided into 81 smaller diamonds—all cut from one pattern.

Make template

Trace diamond pattern for Glittering Star A, page 108, and make template.

Cut fabric

Let's begin by cutting and piecing just one of the large star points. Place template on the wrong side of the fabric and trace. Cut out, adding ¼" to ½" seam allowances:

18 A diamonds of fabric for diamond No. 1
9 A diamonds from each of 7 other fabrics

Assemble star point

Lay all the diamonds, face up, in your color sequence, following Fig. 1. Look carefully and you'll see that the small diamonds can be stitched together to form diagonal rows, and the rows can be stitched together to complete the large diamond. (See *Rows of diamonds*, page 5.)

Start with the upper right row (Fig. 2). Work with pairs of diamonds and stitch them together. Then join the pairs and add diamond No. 8. Trim seam allowances to ⅛" and finger-press all seams in the same direction.

Stitch the remaining rows in the same way, being very careful to watch your color sequence. Try to alternate seam directions in adjoining rows, pressing one row up and the next row down.

When all rows are completed, stitch them together. Trim the seams and finger-press them to one side.

There! You've finished one large star point. Now repeat the same steps to complete seven more for the center of your quilt.

Cut background pieces

You'll have to draft two large templates for the background pieces, and you may need to tape two pieces of poster board together.

For B, measure a 22½" square (Fig. 3). Also draft a separate C triangle with 22½" sides—or wait until you've traced the B square on fabric, then cut the template in half on the diagonal to make the C (Fig. 3).

Place templates on the wrong side of the background fabric. (Keep long side of the triangle

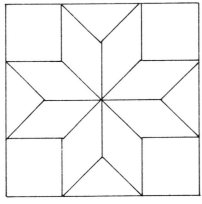

Fig. 4 *Piecing star block*

on the lengthwise grain.) Trace templates. Cut out, adding ¼" to ½" seam allowances:
   4 B squares
   4 C triangles

Assemble large star

As you work, refer to *Piecing diamonds*, page 4.

Lay star points and background squares and triangles, face up, to form the block in Fig. 4. Check Fig. 1 and your color diagram to be sure the correct tip of each star point is at the center of the block.

Stitch the star points together, beginning and ending each seam on the pencil points (do not stitch into seam allowances). Then piece in the squares and triangles.

Isn't that gorgeous?

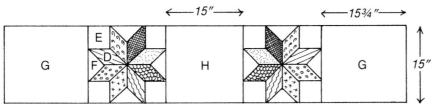

Fig. 5 *Joining top panel*

Make top panel

Five large blocks, including two stars, form the panel.

Make templates

Trace patterns D-F for Eight-Pointed Star, page 109, and make templates. Also draft templates for G, a 15x15¾" rectangle, and H, a 15" square.

Cut fabric

Place templates on the wrong side of the fabric and trace. Cut out, adding ¼" to ½" seam allowances:
   16 D diamonds (2 each of the 8 fabrics used in the large star)
   2 G rectangles of background fabric
   1 H square of background fabric

Assemble small star blocks

Lay pieces, face up, to form two star blocks—just like the large star block (see Fig. 4). Arrange colors so that the stars are mirror images. Stitch star points together as you did for the large star. Then piece in the squares and triangles.

Join panel units

Lay panel pieces, face up, following Fig. 5. Stitch them together.

Complete quilt top

After the large star and top panel are finished, you can add the border strips and join the units.

Cut border pieces

There is a narrow inside border (red on sample) around the large star and top panel, and a larger outside border (black on sample). Make two templates that are the widths of the borders and about 15" long (you can slide the templates along to mark the required lengths). You'll need one template 2" wide and one 4½" wide.

Use the fabric you saved for the borders. Place templates on the wrong side of the fabric, and mark the lengths needed. Cut out, adding ¼" to ½" seam allowances:
   2 strips, 2x93½" each, for inner (red) border
   2 strips, 2x80½" each, for inner (red) border
   1 strip, 2x76½", for inner (red) border
   2 strips, 4½x97½" each, for outside (black) border
   2 strips, 4½x89½" each, for outside (black) border

Add borders

The two sections of the quilt—the giant Glittering Star block and the top panel—are joined by the 2x76½" strip of inner border. First stitch this border strip to the bottom edge of the top panel. Then stitch

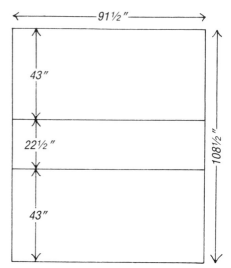

← — 91½″ — →

43″

22½″

43″

108½″

Fig. 6 *Piecing the backing*

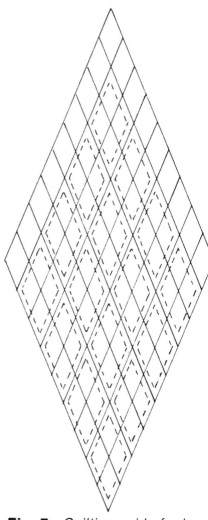

Fig. 7 *Quilting guide for large star point*

the opposite side of the strip to the top edge of the Glittering Star block.

To each long side of the quilt top, add a 2x93½″ inner border strip. Then add a 2x80½″ inner border strip to the top and bottom of the quilt.

Now work with the outside border. Add a 4½x97½″ strip to each side of the quilt. Then add a 4½x89½″ strip to the top and the bottom.

Step back and survey your work with pride.

Finish quilt

See *Quilting the whole top*, page 149. Piece the backing, following Fig. 6 as a guide. Press the quilt top and the backing.

Mark quilting lines
The sample quilt has straight-line quilting, with parallel lines radiating from the Glittering Star. To mark your quilt top for this, begin at seam lines that join the rows of diamonds and extend these lines to form a pattern. See *Marking simple lines and shapes*, page 147.

Quilting guides
Stack the layers, smoothing quilt top over backing and batting. Baste the layers together.

Before you begin stitching, see *Making quilting stitches*, page 148, and *Basic quilting*, page 147. On Glittering Star, begin at the center point. If you don't want to quilt inside each diamond, you can handle four small diamonds in each star point as a unit (Fig. 7).

Quilt lines you have marked on the background fabric.

On the small star blocks, quilt inside each star point.

Finish edges
Make bias from the 36″ square you saved, and stitch bias to the quilt. Follow directions under *Using continuous bias*, page 151.

**GLITTERING STAR
A**

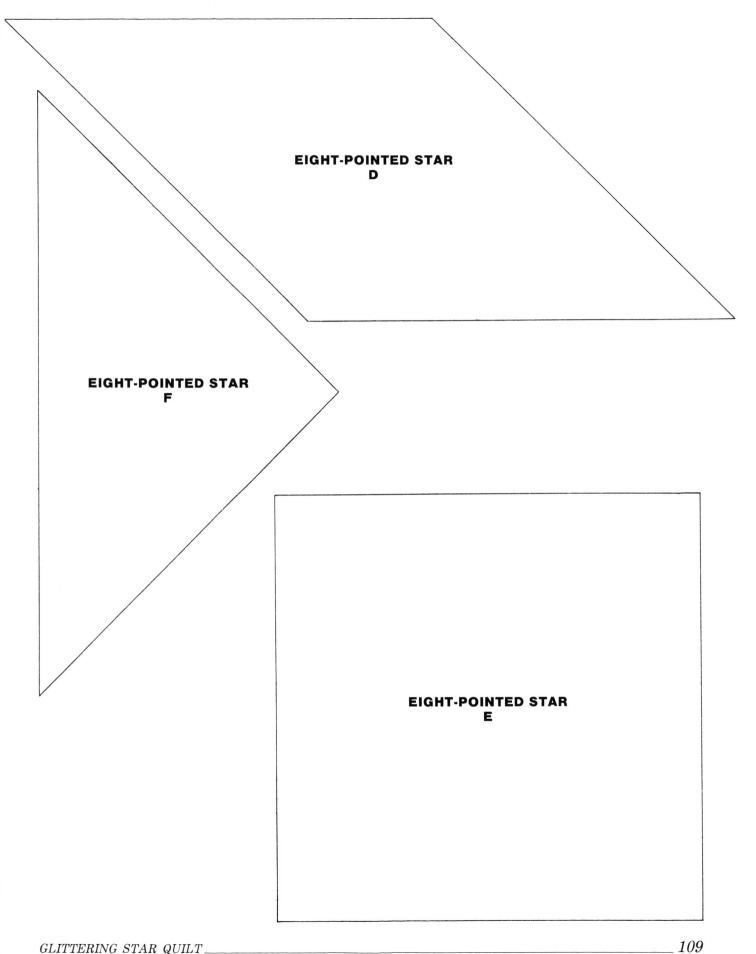

**EIGHT-POINTED STAR
D**

**EIGHT-POINTED STAR
F**

**EIGHT-POINTED STAR
E**

(color photo, page 119)

7

Heavenly Bears Crib Quilt

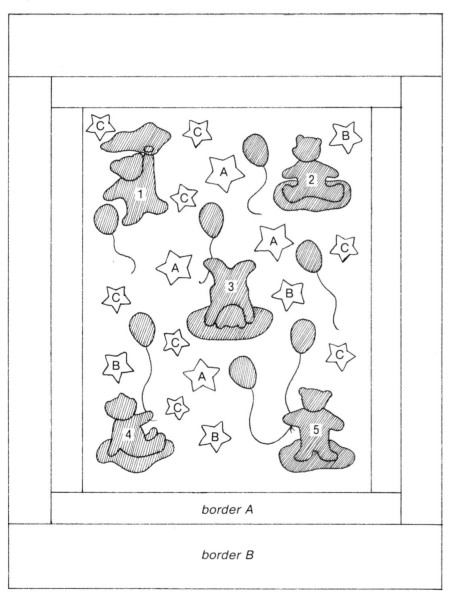

border A

border B

Fig. 1 *Diagram for assembling quilt top*

Here are five little bears, playing with colorful balloons on a sky of quilted stars.

I made each bear of a different tan print, but you could make them all the same. The clouds are lined with polyester fleece, and the balloons are puffed with a little stuffing.

The finished quilt is 41x54", and it could easily be turned into a wall hanging. You also could appliqué just one bear to a 12" square for a pillow top.

Materials
(Yardage is for fabric 45" wide.)

1½ yd. blue fabric with white dots, for center panel and bias binding
½ yd. yellow print, for border A
2¼ yd. red print, for border B and backing
¼ yd. white solid, for clouds
5 scraps of tan prints or solids, for bears
5 scraps of bright prints or solids, for shirts
7 scraps of bright solids, for balloons and letter trim
Thread for piecing borders in white or blending color
Thread for appliqué in matching colors
Quilting thread in white or colors (I used yellow)
Embroidery floss in off-white, brown, tan, black and red
1 pkg. polyester batting, 45x60"
¼ yd. thin polyester fleece, 42" wide, for clouds
Small amount of polyester stuffing, for balloons

Prepare fabric

Prewash all the fabric if you plan to wash the finished quilt. Then cut off sections which will be used later for the backing, center panel and bias binding.

From the red print, cut a 43x56″ section for the backing. From the blue fabric, cut a 24″ square for making bias. Set these sections aside.

On the wrong side of the blue fabric, measure a 27x36″ rectangle. Cut out, adding ¼″ to ½″ seam allowances. This is the center sky panel.

Complete quilt top

For tips on making templates and doing appliqué work, see Chapter 1. Be sure to read *Intricate Shapes*, page 8.

Make templates

Trace patterns for the five bears and clouds, pages 114-118, and the balloon, page 117. (Do not trace embroidery lines for balloon strings, except on bears' paws.) Make one whole template for each bear and its cloud. Make a separate template for the balloon.

Make clouds

Lay the blue center panel on the floor or table, right side up. Position the whole template for each bear and its cloud on the panel, right side up (see Fig. 1). Trace around each template very lightly with a colored pencil. This outline will help you place appliqué pieces later.

Cut each bear away from its cloud. Place each cloud template, face up, on the right side of the white fabric. Trace a whole cloud (do not trace cut-out portion for bear). Cut out, adding ¼″ seam allowance.

Also trace and cut each cloud from fleece, but do not add seam allowance.

Stay-stitch clouds (optional) and clip seam allowances along inside curves. Place matching piece of fleece against wrong side of fabric. Turn seam allowance, baste and press.

Position each cloud on center panel, using your pencil line as a guide. Pin in place.

Add bears

Position each bear template on the panel, overlapping its cloud. Trace portion of bear that is on the cloud. (For Bear No. 1, this will be only a paw.)

Now work with one bear at a time. Cut apart the template for Bear No. 1 to make separate templates for head, arms, shirt and lower body. (You already have the paw.)

Place each template, face up, on the right side of the fabric and trace. Cut out, adding ¼″ seam allowances:

> Head, arms, paw and lower body of tan print or solid
> 1 shirt of bright print or solid

Stay-stitch bear pieces and shirt (optional), and clip seam allowances into V points and inside curves. Turn seam allowances (unless they tuck under other pieces), baste and press.

Position bear on the center panel, using your pencil outlines as a guide. Pin in place.

Cut templates and prepare appliqués for the other four bears in the same manner. For Bear No. 3, also cut a B (or other letter) of bright solid.

Sew all pieces to background, working with bottom layers first. Use matching thread and the appliqué stitch (page 8).

Add balloons

To cut and form balloons, use bright solid colors, and follow directions for *Making perfect circles*, page 7. You'll need 7 balloons.

Position balloons on center panel and pin in place (see Fig. 1). Attach with matching thread and the appliqué stitch, tucking in a little polyester stuffing as you work.

Add design lines

Pencil in embroidery lines for the bears' claws and for the balloon strings. For faces, copy each bear head pattern with face onto tracing paper. Then transfer face lines to matching fabric head; place dressmaker's carbon paper under the tracing and go over the lines with a dry ball-point pen. Use this same method to mark the foot pads on Bear No. 2 and the leg and stomach lines on Bear No. 4.

For bears' eyes and noses, use black embroidery floss and a satin stitch (page 9). On Bears No. 2 and 4, you may want to substitute red floss for the noses to let them show up better against the background fabric.

For claws, use black floss and a straight stitch. For mouths, ears and other design details, use black or brown floss and a chain stitch (page 9). To outline the stomach on Bear No. 4, chain stitch from the embroidered leg line up to the shirt. To outline the letter B on Bear No. 3, use red floss and a chain stitch. Fill inside spaces of the B with a few satin stitches. For balloon strings, use white floss and a chain stitch.

Cut border pieces

Make border templates, each about 15″ long. You'll need three—3″ wide, 4″ wide and 6″ wide. Place templates on the wrong side of the fabric and trace (slide templates along to mark the required lengths). Cut out, adding ¼″ to ½″ seam allowances:

> 2 pieces, 3x36″ each, of yellow print, for border A
> 2 pieces, 3x33″ each, of yellow print, for border A
> 2 pieces, 4x42″ each, of red print, for border B
> 2 pieces, 6x41″ each, of red print, for border B

Add borders

Work with border A (Fig. 1). First add the long strips to each side of the center panel, trim seams and press toward the dark side. Then add the top and bottom strips.

Repeat steps with border B, first adding side strips, then the top and bottom.

The outside edges of the quilt are marked on the wrong side of each border section. To transfer these guidelines to the right side, baste over the pencil lines.

Finish quilt

See *Quilting the whole top*, page 149. Press the quilt top and the backing fabric.

Mark quilting lines

Trace quilting patterns for stars A, B and C, this page, and make templates. For general directions, see *Marking simple lines and shapes*, page 147. Position star templates on sky panel (see Fig. 1) and trace lightly around them.

Quilting guides

Stack the layers, smoothing quilt top over backing and batting. Baste the layers together.

Before you begin stitching, see *Making quilting stitches*, page 148.

Quilt around each bear, cloud, balloon and balloon string, ¼" from seam and embroidery lines. Also quilt lines you marked for the stars.

On sky panel, quilt around edges ¼" from seam lines. On red border, quilt ¼" from inside seam lines and ¼" from outside basting lines.

Finish edges

Make bias from the 24" square of blue fabric, and stitch the bias to the quilt. Follow directions under *Using continuous bias*, page 151.

HEAVENLY BEARS
star quilting designs

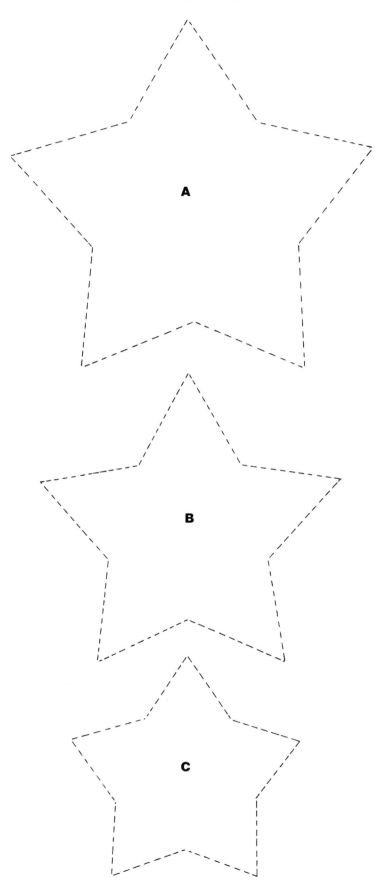

A

B

C

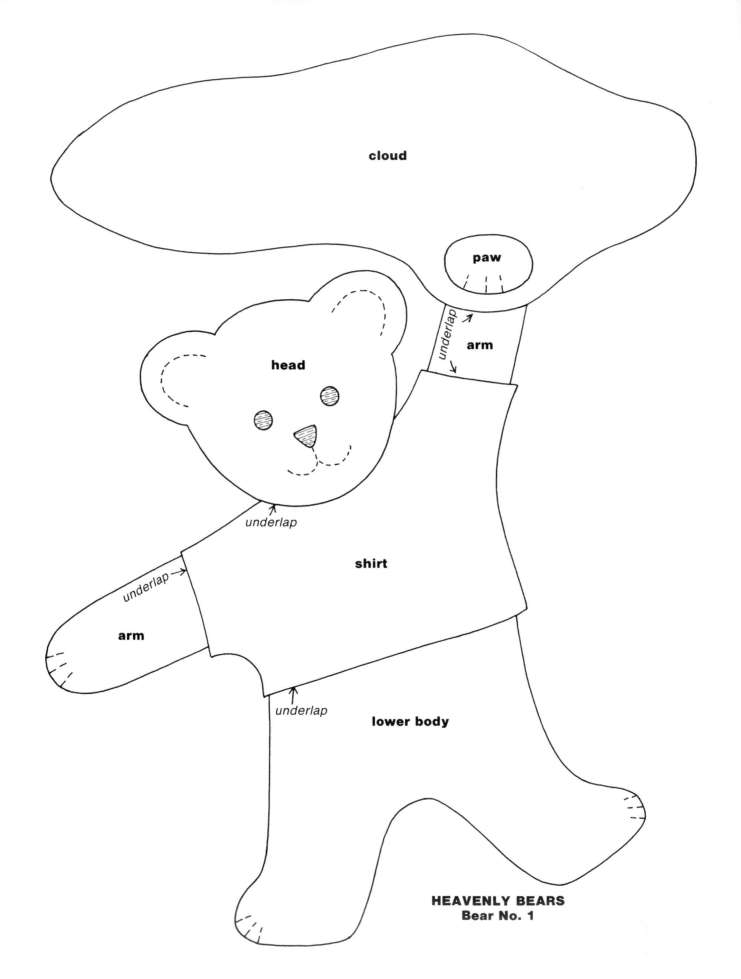

cloud

paw

head

arm

underlap

shirt

underlap

underlap

arm

underlap

lower body

HEAVENLY BEARS
Bear No. 1

*short broken lines
are embroidery lines*

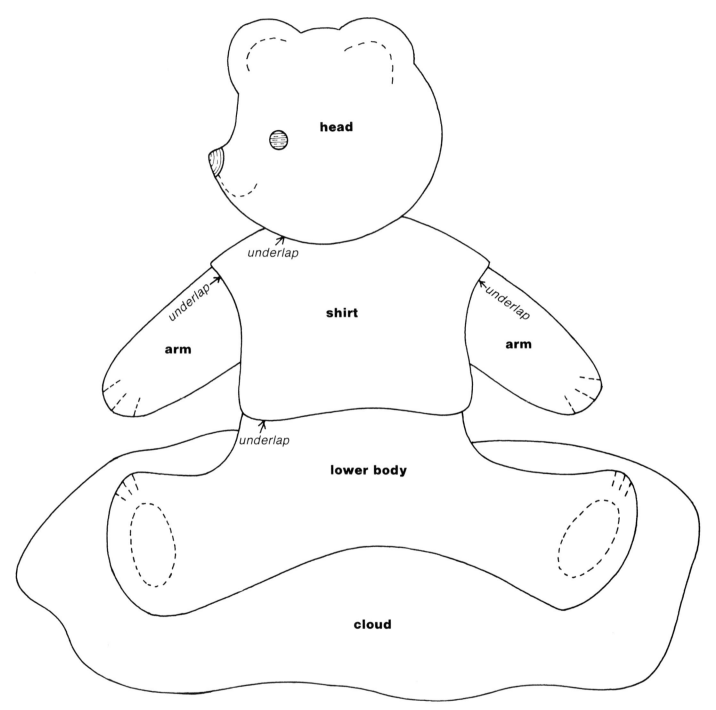

head

underlap

underlap

shirt

underlap

arm

arm

underlap

lower body

cloud

HEAVENLY BEARS
Bear No. 2

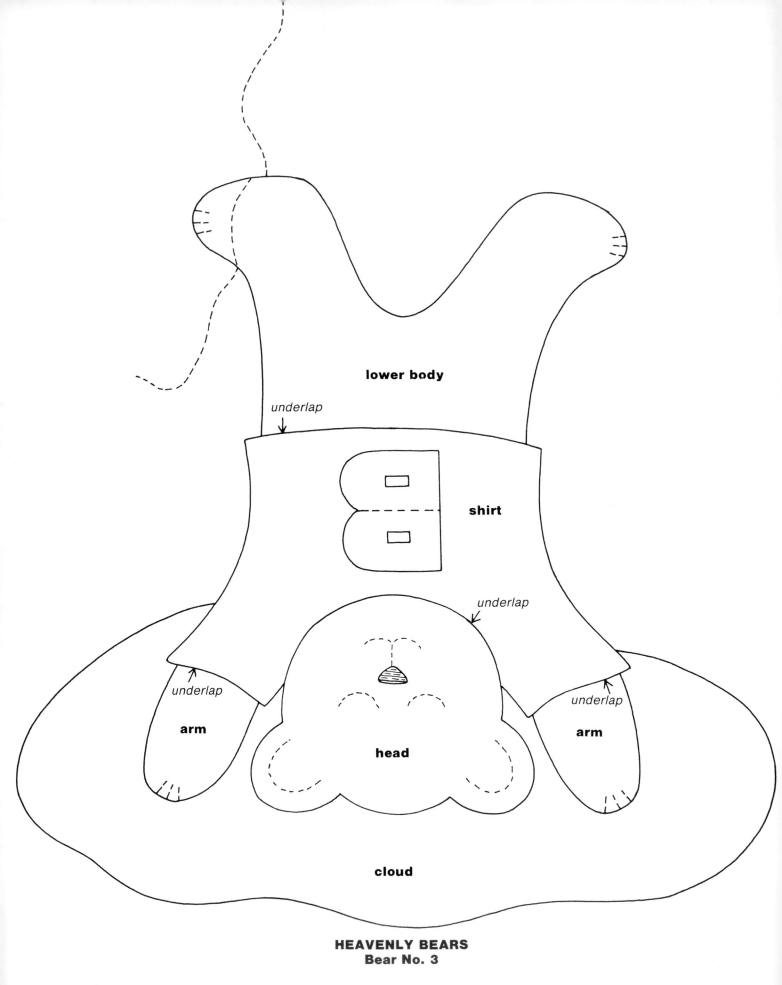

lower body

underlap

shirt

underlap

underlap

arm

head

arm

underlap

cloud

HEAVENLY BEARS
Bear No. 3

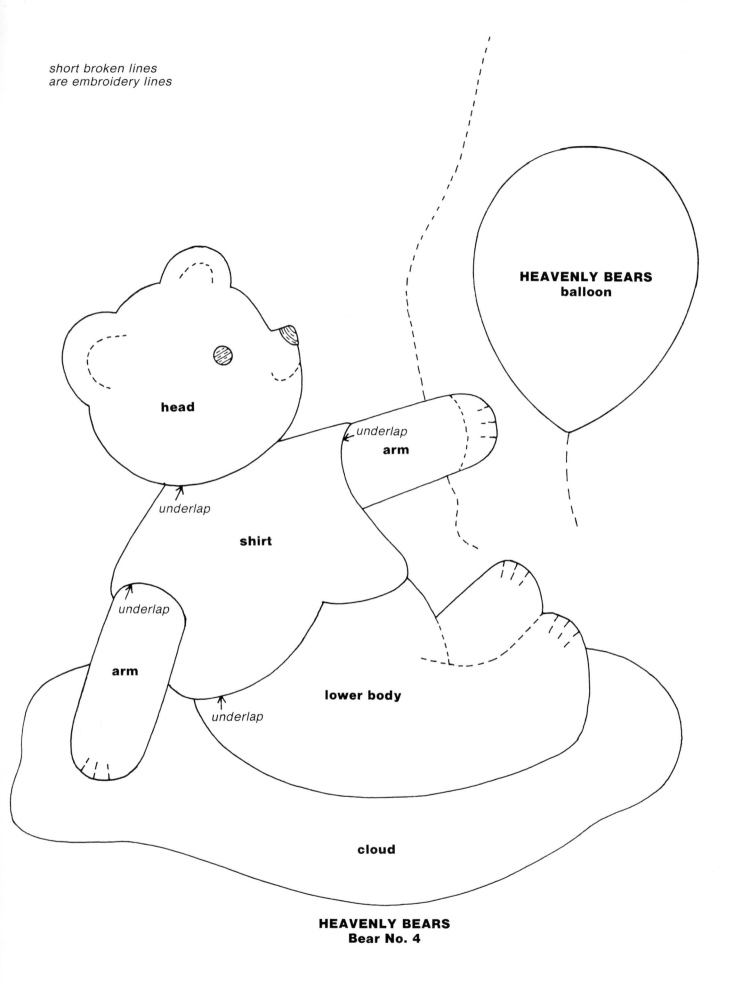

*short broken lines
are embroidery lines*

HEAVENLY BEARS
balloon

head

underlap
arm

underlap

shirt

underlap

arm

underlap

lower body

cloud

HEAVENLY BEARS
Bear No. 4

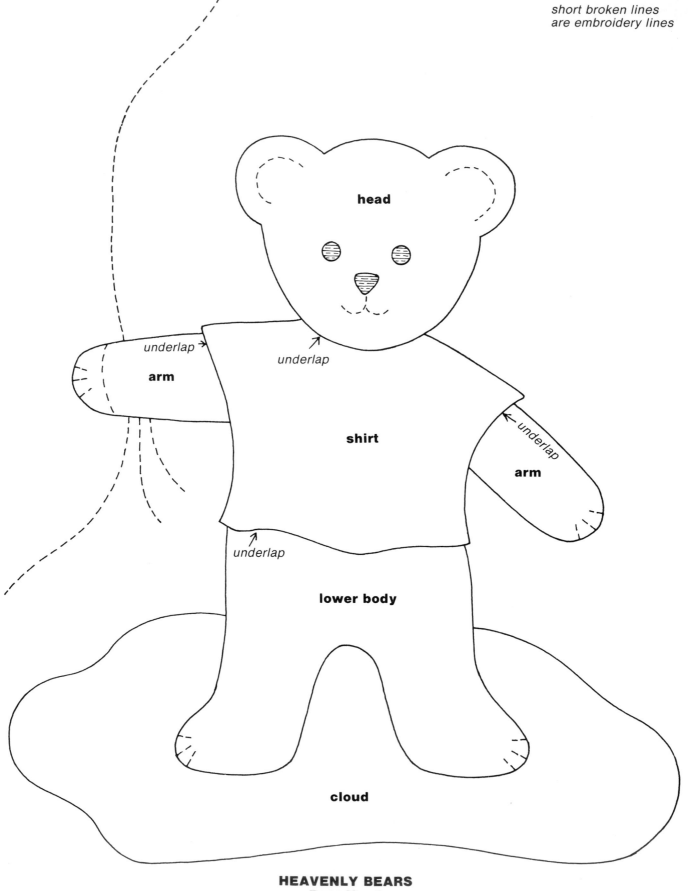

*short broken lines
are embroidery lines*

head

underlap →

underlap

arm

shirt

underlap

arm

underlap

lower body

cloud

HEAVENLY BEARS
Bear No. 5

It was through her church bazaar that she realized she had a saleable product. The things she made sold fast. Long after the bazaar was over her phone kept ringing. "Could I make one more doll, place mat, pillow . . . what have you. It was driving me crazy," she reminisced. In her no-nonsense, true-grit fashion, she found an old cupboard at a junk yard. "I painted it bright red, stuck it in the dining room and filled it with whatever I had time to make," she said. "On thursdays I held open house and friends would come by. By 5 o' clock in the afternoon I was wiped out. My cupboard was bare! It was fun, but unending. That's when the magazine found me."

There's not much time these days for replenishing the shelves of the old red cupboard, although Margaret gets more done than most people.

For artisans who find it difficult to complete projects, we offer her solution. The lights in her cozy workshop go on at 4:30 a.m.! *Why* do you get up so early?" we asked. "Nobody calls at 4:30 in the morning," she laughed. "Think of the work I get done between 4:30 and 7:30, when the phone starts ringing."
Instructions for Crazy Quilt Throw (shown below) begin on page 40.

On facing page: Margaret's love for quilts is evident in the decor of her small elegant house. "Mother and I started making quilts twenty-five years ago, and I had them all over my house before it was the fashionable thing to do!" Her off-white bedroom is a perfect backdrop for the graphics and colors of her collection of quilts. Over the bed is an antique Log Cabin design . . . on the beds, Clay's Choice and a light and dark Log Cabin. Curtains and pillow shams are made of unbleached domestic. At right: In the living room is a colorful collection of things American . . . "I love them because they go so well with quilts!" On the antique blanket chest are thread spool candle holders, and an old basket filled with baby's breath . . . the hooked rug was a gift from her talented neighbor, rug maker Veo Scott, and the hanging was custom made by Margaret for the spot. On the Windsor chair is a lightweight patchwork throw (detail shown above) . . . made from projects gone by — and feather stitched together . . . Instructions for Crazy Quilt throw are on page 40.

HOW TO
Make a Crazy Quilt Throw

Shown on page 39

You will need for 43 x 54-inch throw: 1½ yards lightweight cotton batiste, 1½ yards cotton print backing, calico scraps with as many different designs as possible, black embroidery thread, needle, sewing machine and thread.

Cut a rectangle 41 x 52 inches from the cotton batiste. Cut a large number of calico scraps into any shapes desired. Lay them out and consider color combinations before sewing.

Place a patch in lower left corner. Baste patch all around. Do not turn edges under. Place the second patch, right side down, over first patch, aligning one edge. Use machine and stitch the aligned edge with a narrow seam, sewing through the foundation as well. Open up the second patch. Press flat with right side up. Place third patch, right side down, over patches 1 and 2 or part of them. Sew through all layers as before. Open up, press and repeat with remaining patches. Each raw edge is covered by the sewn edge of the adjoining piece and the work is built out and around until the whole throw is covered. The patches need not have straight edges or be the same size. Adjust each seam curve and length as you go, trimming if necessary. Some raw edges may need to be turned in and blind stitched on top.

Cut calico for backing 42¼ x 53¼ inches which will allow 1¼ inches all around for border. Place backing wrong side up and finished crazy patches over this, right side up. Turn 1¼ inch of print backing to front. Turn raw edges under for ¼-inch hem. Miter corners.

Embroider this border edge and all edges of calico pieces with feather stitch using 3-strand black embroidery

FEATHER STITCH

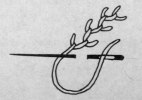

floss. Top may be embroidered before joining to back if desired.

With backing side up, tack front to back every 6 inches using embroidery thread. Be sure to embroider your name and date.

DECORATING & CRAFT IDEAS

Heavenly Bears Crib Quilt

Stained Glass Roses Wall Hanging, page 141

Amish Star Wall Hanging, page 133

8 Lady Jane and Fishing Boy Crib Quilts

People are always looking for crib quilt ideas, and these two quilts are easy to make. Each is just a series of five borders, with a center rectangle and oval. Appliqués decorate the center oval and the second border. To finish the edge, the outside border is turned and hemmed to the backing.

Each finished quilt is 39x50". The design is stitched together, and then the whole top is quilted as one unit.

Lady Jane is done in shades of blue, rose and green, with off-white. Fishing Boy is made in yellow and brown. You can use these colors or substitute your own.

Materials
(Yardage is for fabric 45" wide.)

For Lady Jane:
1 yd. off-white solid, for center rectangle and border B
1 yd. rose print, for borders A and E
½ yd. blue print, for border C and appliqués
½ yd. off-white print, for border D and appliqués
⅓ yd. light green solid, for center oval and leaves
¼ yd. medium green print, for leaves
¼ yd. rose solid, for hat and flower centers
Black solid scrap, for shoes
1½ yd. print or solid, for backing
½ yd. lace, ¼" wide, for trim

1 pkg. dark green double-fold bias tape (3 yd.), for vine
Thread for piecing in white or blending color
Thread for appliqué in matching colors
Quilting thread in white or colors
White embroidery floss
1 pkg. polyester batting, 45x60"

For Fishing Boy:
1 yd. yellow solid or soft print, for center rectangle and border B
1 yd. brown print, for borders A and E
¾ yd. orange with small dots, for center oval, border C and a fish appliqué
½ yd. beige print, for border D and boy's shirt
Scraps: tan print for hat, brown solid for pants, black solid for shoes, gray print for bucket, peach solid for hands, assorted fabrics for fish
1½ yd. print or solid, for backing
Thread for piecing in white or blending color
Thread for appliqué in matching colors
Quilting thread in white or colors
Embroidery floss in brown, orange, yellow and tan
1 pkg. polyester batting, 45x60"

Prepare fabric

Prewash all the fabric if you plan to wash the finished quilt. Then cut as follows.

For Lady Jane: From the off-white print, cut 5" along one cut edge (across the width of fabric). From the blue print, cut 6" along one cut edge (across the width of fabric). Use these small strips for appliqué pieces; set aside larger sections for borders.

For Fishing Boy: From beige print (for border D), cut a 6" square. Use this square for boy's shirt; set aside larger section for border.

Assemble quilt top

For tips on making templates and doing appliqué work, see Chapter 1. Be sure to read *Intricate Shapes*, page 8.

Make templates
Trace half pattern for oval, page 129, to make a full pattern. To do this, fold paper in half, then open paper and place fold over broken line. Trace oval half, refold paper and cut out full pattern.

From poster board, make a template for a rectangle 14x17". On top of template, center the oval and trace around it. Cut out the oval, leaving the rectangle with a center opening.

Fig. 1 *Whole template for Fishing Boy*

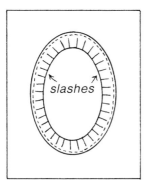

Fig. 2 *Preparing center oval*

Fig. 3 *Cutting Lady Jane template apart*

Fig. 4 *Cutting Fishing Boy template apart*

Now make the appliqué templates.

For Lady Jane: Trace pattern for Lady Jane, page 128, and make a whole template. Also trace leaf and flower hexagon, and make templates.

For Fishing Boy: Trace pattern for Fishing Boy (including bucket, fishing pole and line), page 130, and make a whole template (Fig. 1). Also trace fish A-D, page 131, and make templates.

Begin with center section

Place the rectangle template on the wrong side of the fabric (off-white for Lady Jane or yellow for Fishing Boy), keeping edges on the straight grain. Trace rectangle and oval. Then cut out the rectangle only, adding ¼" to ½" seam allowances.

Stay-stitch just inside the oval marking, then cut out the oval center, leaving a ¼" seam allowance. Slash to the stay-stitching (Fig. 2). Turn the raw edge to the wrong side and baste. You have just made a frame!

Now to fill in the oval. On the wrong side of the fabric (light green for Lady Jane or orange with dots for Fishing Boy), mark a rectangle 10x13" and cut out on the pencil line. Center this, right side up, under the oval opening and pin.

Sew in place, using matching thread and an appliqué stitch (page 8). Trim seam allowance to ¼". Now we're ready to dress dolls.

Prepare appliqués

Center the whole template of Lady Jane or Fishing Boy on the fabric oval and trace around it very lightly. This outline will help you to place appliqué pieces.

Now cut the whole template apart to make individual templates (Figs. 3 and 4). Place each template piece, face up, on the right side of the fabric and trace. Cut out, adding ¼" seam allowances.

For Lady Jane, you need:
Dress top, bottom and sleeves of blue print
Pinafore of white print
Pantaloons of white print
Hatband of blue print
2 shoes of black solid
To cut and form bonnet, use rose solid fabric and follow the directions for *Making perfect circles*, page 7.

For Fishing Boy, you need:
Shirt of tan print
Pants of brown solid
2 shoes of black solid
Bucket of gray print or solid
To cut and form hat, use beige print and follow the directions for *Making perfect circles*, page 7.

To make boy's hands, fold a piece of peach fabric, right side inside. Trace around each hand, but do not cut. Stitch around the curve on each hand, leaving straight edge open. Cut out; leave a ⅛" seam allowance along curve and a ¼" seam allowance on the straight edge. Turn to right side. You have two nice, neat hands. (Raw edges will tuck under shirt sleeves.)

Position pieces

Stay-stitch appliqué pieces (optional) and clip seam allowances into V points and inside curves. Turn seam allowances (unless they tuck under another piece), baste and press.

Position appliqué pieces on oval, using your pencil outline as a guide. Pin in place. Now add straps to clothing.

For Lady Jane: To make pinafore straps, cut a ¾x4" strip of white print. With right side out, fold both lengthwise edges of strip to overlap at center and press. Cut strip in half to make two ¼x2" strips. Place straps on dress top; tuck bottom edges under pinafore and top edges under bonnet.

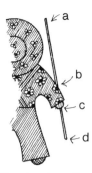

Fig. 5 *Beginning the couching stitch*

Fig. 6 *Finishing couching stitch*

For Fishing Boy: To make suspenders, cut a ¾x7½" strip of brown solid. With right side out, fold both lengthwise edges of strip to overlap at center and press. Cut strip in half to make two ¼x3¾" strips. Place strips, crossed, on shirt; tuck bottom edges under pants and top edges under hat.

Appliqué

Sew pieces in place, beginning with bottom layers. Use matching thread and the appliqué stitch (page 8). Then add trimmings.

For Lady Jane: To make bow for bonnet, cut a 2x9" strip of blue print. Fold in half lengthwise, right side inside, and stitch a narrow seam. Turn strip to right side, center seam on one side of strip and press. Cut off 2" and set aside. Fold longer strip so that each end overlaps the center of the strip by ½"; sew across center to gather. Cover gathering line with the 2" strip, overlapping raw edges in back; tack to hold. Position bow on hatband and sew in place.

Position lace along curved edge of pinafore, bottom curve of dress and bottom edge of pantaloons. Tuck cut ends under and sew lace in place.

To mark center line on pantaloons, use white embroidery floss and a few chain stitches (page 9).

For Fishing Boy: To mark hatband line for embroidery, cut center circle away from hat to use as a template. Center template on hat appliqué and trace. Then embroider line with brown floss and a chain stitch (page 9). Add a decorative edge to the hat with brown floss and a blanket stitch (page 9).

To form the bucket handle and outline the pants pocket, use tan floss and a chain stitch.

The fishing pole is worked in a couching stitch to suggest a bamboo pole. Use six strands of tan floss in an embroidery

needle; knot one end. Bring needle up from back of fabric at top of fishing pole (Fig. 5, a). Take one long stitch to cover pencil line and go back into fabric at sleeve (b). Come out below hand (c) and take floss down to bottom of pole (d); secure thread on back of fabric.

To hold the long stitches in place, thread needle with two strands of brown embroidery floss and knot one end. Bring needle up from back of fabric at top of pole. Take one stitch over pole, go back into fabric and come up for next stitch a short distance ahead (Fig. 6). Continue taking single stitches all along pole.

For the fishing line, use two strands of brown floss and a chain stitch.

Cut borders

Make templates that are the widths of the border pieces and about 15" long (you can slide the templates along to mark the required lengths). You'll need six templates—1½" wide, 2" wide, 3" wide, 4" wide, 5" wide and 6" wide.

Place templates on the wrong side of the fabric, trace and label. Cut out, adding ¼" to ½" seam allowances:

- 4 pieces, 1½x17" each, for border A (rose print for Lady Jane or brown print for Fishing Boy)
- 2 pieces, 6x25" each, and 2 pieces, 4x20" each, for border B (off-white for Lady Jane or yellow for Fishing Boy)
- 2 pieces, 2x32" each, and 2 pieces, 2x29" each, for border C (blue print for Lady Jane or orange with dots for Fishing Boy)
- 2 pieces, 2x36" each, and 2 pieces, 2x33" each, for border D (off-white print for Lady Jane or beige print for Fishing Boy)

Border E, on the outside, will be folded to the back to finish the edges, so extra fabric for turning is needed. (Use rose

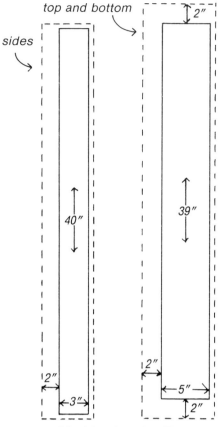

Fig. 7 *Marking border E*

print for Lady Jane or brown print for Fishing Boy.) For sides, mark 2 pieces, 3x40" each. Add 2" for turning and seam allowance on one long (40") edge, and add ¼" to ½" seam allowance on all other edges (Fig. 7).

For border E top and bottom, mark 2 pieces, 5x39" each. Add 2" for turning and seam allowances on one long (39") edge and on each short edge, and add a ¼" to ½" seam allowance on the remaining long edge.

Cut out the four border E pieces.

Add borders A, B and C

Work from the center out, beginning with border A. Add the sides first, then the top and bottom (Fig. 8).

Repeat step with border B pieces, and then with border C pieces.

Add border appliqués

Before you go any further, add the appliqués to border B.

For Lady Jane: The stylized flowers are made by the English piecing method (see page 6). Use the hexagon flower template to make paper patterns for 28 flower pieces.

Pin paper templates to wrong side of the fabric. Cut out fabric, adding at least ¼" seam allowances. For each flower, you need:

6 hexagons of blue print
1 hexagon of rose, for flower center

Fold fabric over paper and baste. Join pieces with a whipping stitch (page 6) to form flower. Press, remove bastings and pop the papers.

Complete four flowers, center one in each corner of border B and pin in place.

To draw the connecting vine, trace the vine pattern, page 129, and transfer it to the center of both the 4"-wide border template and the 6"-wide border template. Make the final lines heavy. Position

each template under matching border piece, with center of vine at center of border (see photo, page 122). Use a pencil to trace the line onto the border, moving template along in both directions until the vine meets the corner flowers.

Lay green bias tape over lines for the vine, connecting flowers and tucking raw ends of bias under flowers. Pin in place.

Form the leaves, following directions for *Making perfect circles*, page 7. You'll need:

14 leaves of green solid
14 leaves of green print

Pin the leaves in place (see photo), with print leaves along inner edge of vine and solid green leaves along outer edge of vine. Sew flowers, vine and leaves to the border, using matching thread and the appliqué stitch.

For Fishing Boy: Place fish templates, face up, on right side of print fabrics and trace. Cut out, adding ¼" seam allowances:

2 fish A
1 fish A (reversed)
2 fish B
2 fish B (reversed)
2 fish C
2 fish C (reversed)
1 fish D

Stay-stitch each fish (optional), clip seam allowances into V points and inside curves. Turn seam allowances, baste and press.

Position fish on border B (see Fig. 8). Sew in place, using matching thread and the appliqué stitch. To embellish edges, use contrasting floss and a blanket stitch.

Pencil in embroidery lines for fish mouths, for fins on fish A and for waterspout above fish D. Embroider lines with contrasting floss and a chain stitch.

To make each fish eye, use a coin for a template (a quarter for fish A and D, and a nickel for fish B and C). Trace coin on contrasting color fabric and cut

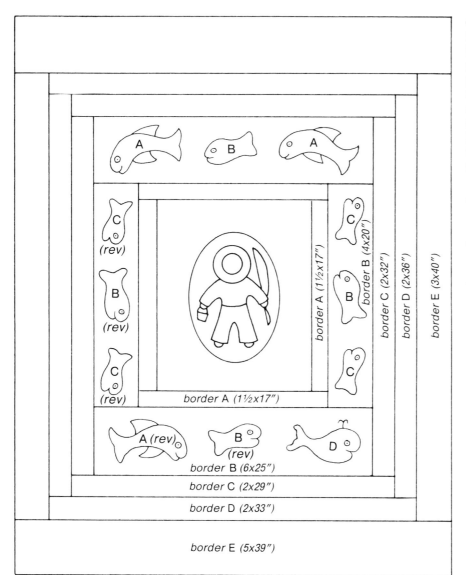

Fig. 8 *Guide for assembling crib quilt (and for placing fish appliqués on Fishing Boy quilt)*

out on pencil line. Make a running stitch around the edge of fabric circle. Draw thread, gathering edge until you have a plump little circle. Flatten circle with your finger, hiding the raw edge underneath. Position eye on fish and appliqué in place. For center of eye, use contrasting floss and a French knot (page 9).

Add borders D and E
Pin and stitch border D to border C, first adding the sides and then the top and bottom pieces.

Add border E, first stitching the sides and then the top and bottom pieces.

To transfer lines for outside edges of quilt to the right side of the fabric, baste along your pencil lines on border E. You will have 2″ of fabric extending beyond these lines.

Finish quilt

See *Quilting the whole top*, page 149. From backing fabric, cut a section 39x50″. Press the quilt top and the backing.

Mark quilting lines
Mark diagonal lines to crisscross on center rectangle (skipping over center oval); draw lines from corner to corner, then place additional lines 1¾″ apart.

Quilting guides
Stack the layers, smoothing quilt top over backing and batting. Baste the layers together.

Before you begin stitching, see *Making quilting stitches*, page 148. Quilt pieced work and appliqués following guides under *Basic quilting*, page 147. On center rectangle, quilt diagonal lines you marked. On border E, quilt outside edge ¼″ from basting (turning) line.

Finish edges
Follow directions for *Folding border over edges*, page 151.

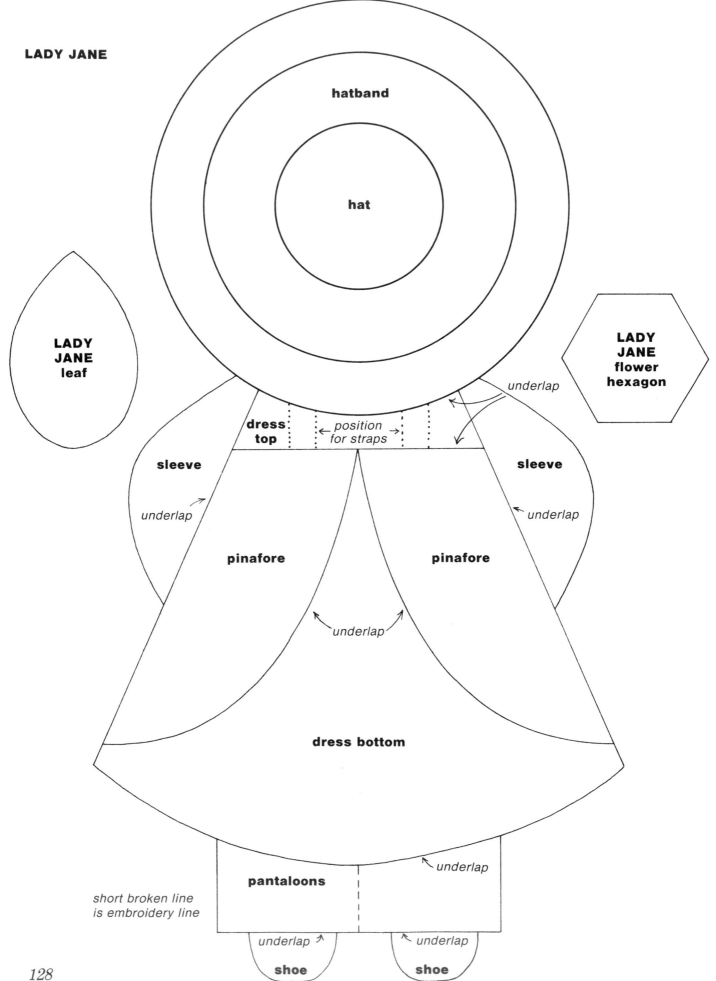

LADY JANE

hatband

hat

LADY
JANE
leaf

LADY
JANE
flower
hexagon

underlap

dress
top

← *position
for straps* →

sleeve

sleeve

underlap

underlap

pinafore

pinafore

underlap

dress bottom

underlap

pantaloons

*short broken line
is embroidery line*

underlap ↗

↖ *underlap*

shoe

shoe

128

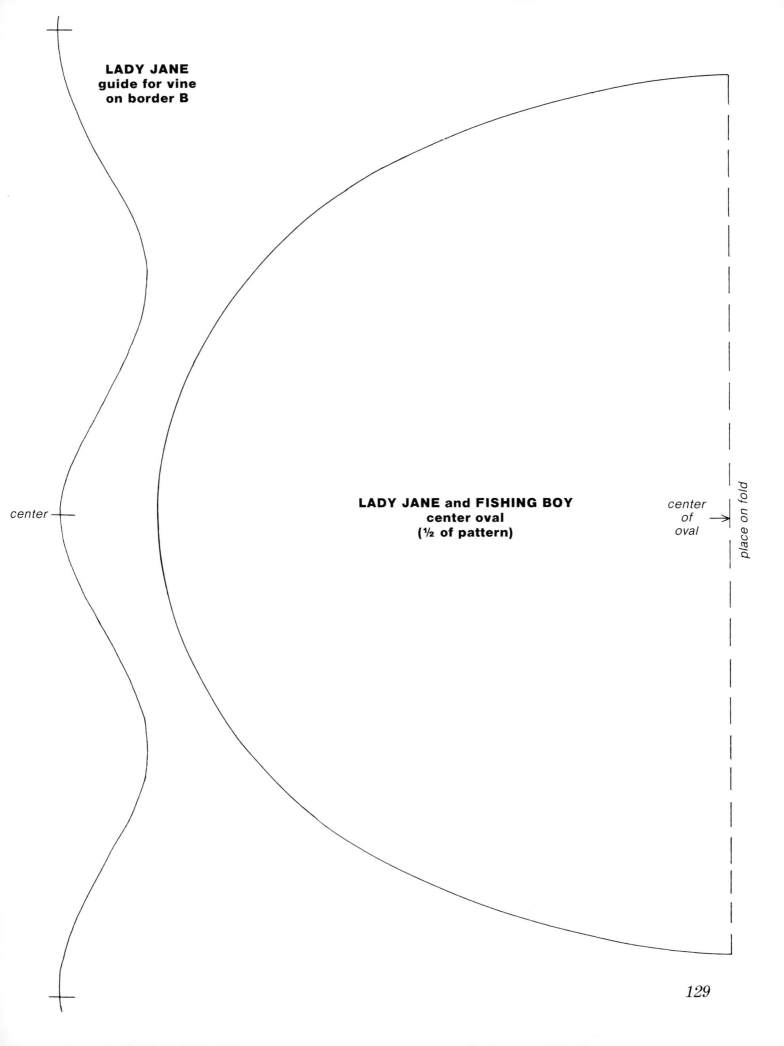

LADY JANE
guide for vine
on border B

center

LADY JANE and FISHING BOY
center oval
(½ of pattern)

center
of
oval

place on fold

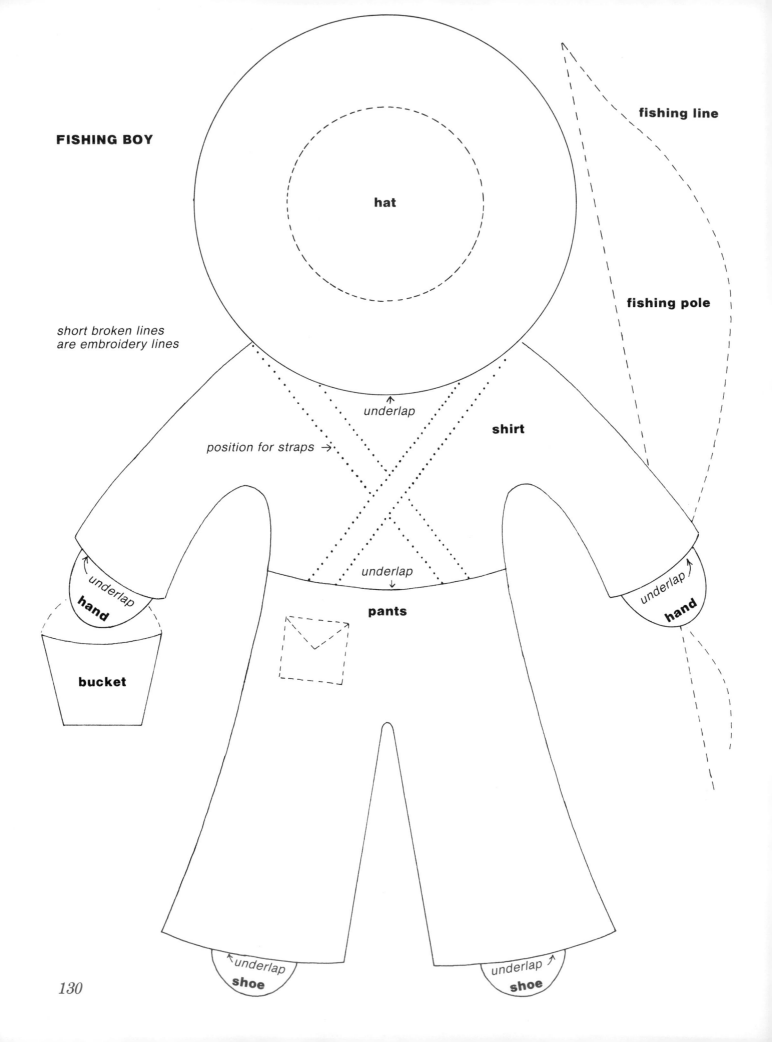

FISHING BOY

hat

fishing line

fishing pole

*short broken lines
are embroidery lines*

underlap

shirt

position for straps →

underlap

underlap

hand

pants

underlap

hand

bucket

underlap

shoe

underlap

shoe

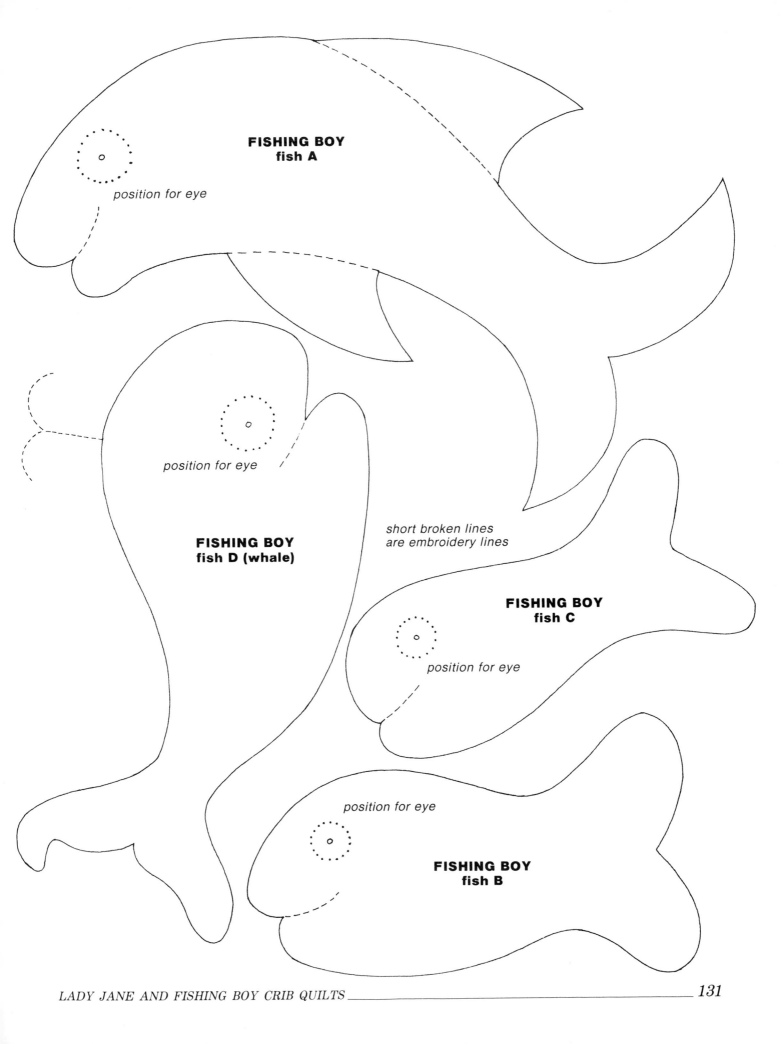

FISHING BOY
fish A

position for eye

position for eye

FISHING BOY
fish D (whale)

short broken lines
are embroidery lines

FISHING BOY
fish C

position for eye

position for eye

FISHING BOY
fish B

border No. 1
border No. 2
border No. 3
border No. 4

(color photo, page 121)

9 Amish Star Wall Hanging

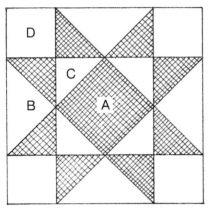

Fig. 1 *VARIABLE STAR*

Some of the most highly prized antique quilts are those done by the Amish. Their simply pieced designs in strong solid colors are truly magnificent.

After seeing some of these quilts, practically every quilter wants to make something "kind of Amish." My class members are no exception, so I presented this wall hanging as an idea for them. Maybe you'll enjoy making it, too.

I chose to do this one in red, moss green, aqua and, of course, black. You may prefer other colors, but do include black or some very dark color.

The complete design is stitched together, and then the whole top is quilted as one unit. The finished piece is 38" square.

Materials
(Yardage is for fabric 45" wide.)

1 yd. red solid, for piecing and bias binding
¾ yd. black solid
½ yd. aqua solid
¼ yd. moss green solid
1¼ yd. solid or print, for backing
Thread for piecing in blending color
Black quilting thread
1 pkg. polyester batting, 45x60"

Prepare fabric

Prewash all the fabric if you plan to wash the finished wall hanging. From red, cut a 24" square for continuous bias and set aside to use later.

Complete quilt top

For tips on making templates and piecing, see Chapter 1.

Make templates
Trace patterns A-F, page 145, and make templates. Also draft border templates, each about 15" long. You'll need three—1" wide, 2" wide and 3" wide.

Cut borders and center star
Let's start by making the center block, which is called Variable Star, and then surround it with two borders. (We'll cut pieces for all four borders first, then you can cut smaller shapes from the leftover fabric.)

Place templates on the wrong side of the fabric and trace. For long border pieces, you can slide the templates along to mark the required lengths. Cut out fabric, adding ¼" to ½" seam allowances.

For the borders, you need:
    4 strips, 3x32" each, of black, for border No. 4
    2 strips, 1x14" each, of black, for border No. 1
    2 strips, 1x12" each, of black, for border No. 1
    4 strips, 2x14" each, of aqua, for border No. 2
    4 E squares of green, for border No. 2
    4 D squares of aqua, for border No. 4
    2 strips, 1x32" each, of red, for border No. 3
    2 strips, 1x30" each, of red, for border No. 3
For the center Variable Star, you need:
    1 A square of red
    4 B triangles of green
    8 C triangles of red
    4 C triangles of green
    4 D squares of green

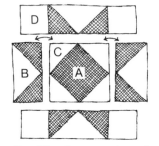

Fig. 2 *Piecing center star*

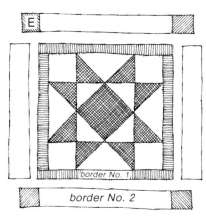

Fig. 3 *Adding borders*

Assemble center star

Lay all pieces, face up, to form the block in Fig. 1. Pin-baste and stitch a green C triangle to each side of the red A square, forming a larger square. (Be sure to match pencil lines and end points.) Trim seams and finger-press to one side.

Add a red C triangle to each short side of the four green B triangles. This forms four rectangles.

Now we want to make rows. Add two green D squares to each end of the top and bottom rectangles (Fig. 2). Stitch the side rectangles to the center square to form a center row. Then sew the three rows together, being careful to match seam lines. The center block is all done!

Add two borders

To add border No. 1, pin-baste and stitch a 1x12″ black piece to both sides of the Variable Star block (Fig. 3). Trim each seam and finger-press to the black side. Then add a 1x14″ black piece to the top and bottom of the star block.

To add border No. 2, stitch an aqua rectangle to both sides of the center square. This forms a center row. Add a green E square to each end of the remaining two aqua rectangles to form a top and bottom row. Then sew the three rows together.

So far, so good.

Cut small star pieces

Now, we must make a group of smaller star blocks, all in a pieced design called Ohio Star (Fig. 4). You will need four blocks in red, six in aqua and six in green.

Place templates on the wrong side of the fabric and trace. Cut out, adding ¼″ to ½″ seam allowances:

    4 E squares of red
    6 E squares of green
    6 E squares of aqua
    64 E squares of black
    32 F triangles of red
    48 F triangles of green
    48 F triangles of aqua
    128 F triangles of black

Assemble small stars

Start by pin-basting and sewing each colored F triangle to a black F triangle along a short side. If you use a machine, feed the triangles, a pair at a time, under the presser foot to stitch the seams. Don't cut the thread between the pairs until you are done. (It's like making a tail for a kite.) Then snip the pairs apart, finger-press the seams to the black side, and separate the colors.

Let's make a red block first. Line up pieces to form the block in Fig. 4, with a red E square in the center and four black E squares at the corners. Position the red/black triangle units you stitched so that they follow the design.

Stitch the triangle units together to form squares. Then join squares to form three horizontal rows. Finally, stitch the rows together to complete the block.

Now that you've made one, the rest should be easy. Just keep going until you have all 16 blocks.

Arrange the small blocks around the large center unit, following photo on page 121 for color placement. Join the five blocks along the top and along the bottom to form two horizontal rows.

Join the remaining three blocks on each side to form

Fig. 4 *OHIO STAR*

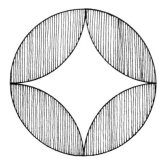

Fig. 5 *Quilting template for square*

Fig. 6 *Quilting template for B triangle*

two vertical rows. Then stitch these vertical rows to the center unit, and you have another horizontal row.

Join the three horizontal rows to form a big square.

Add last two borders

For border No. 3, add a 1x30″ red piece to both sides of the large center square (see photo, page 132). Then add a 1x32″ red piece to the top and bottom.

Work on border No. 4 by stitching a black strip to both sides of the center unit to form a center row. Add an aqua D square to each end of the top and bottom black pieces, forming rows. Then sew the rows together to complete the design.

To transfer lines for the outside edges of the quilt to the right side of the border, baste over your pencil lines.

Finish quilt

See *Quilting the whole top*, page 149. Mark a 40″ square on the backing fabric and cut out. Press the backing and the pieced quilt top.

Mark quilting lines

Old Amish quilts are famous for their very beautiful and involved quilting. The designs I'm offering you are a lot simpler, but still effective when quilted with black thread.

Make templates for quilting designs from patterns on page 145; use plastic or poster board.

For the squares A, D and E, the quilting templates will be circles with cut-out centers (Fig. 5); leave a little bridge at each connecting point on the circles so the templates hold together. Center each design on the appropriate fabric square and trace with a No. 5H or 6H pencil.

For B triangles, copy flower design and make template. Carefully cut away the inside petal (Fig. 6). Position and trace

the outside petals, then position and trace the inside petal.

To mark the quilting design on border No. 2 (aqua), center the oval template at one end of an aqua strip and trace. Move and trace the template to the other end, so that you have seven evenly spaced ovals. Repeat to mark the three other aqua border strips.

Quilting guides

Stack the layers, smoothing quilt top over backing and batting. Baste the layers together.

Before you begin stitching, see *Making quilting stitches*, page 148. Start at the center and use black quilting thread. Quilt designs you have marked. On other pieces with no special design, quilt inside each shape, ¼″ from seam lines.

Finish edges

Make bias from the 24″ square of red fabric, and stitch bias to the quilt. Follow directions under *Using continuous bias*, page 151.

When you trim the outside edges of the quilt layers, leave ½″ seam allowances beyond your basting lines. (The backing and batting can be this wide, even if the quilt top is narrower.) This ½″ will be your guide when adding the bias.

Add fabric for hanging

Follow directions under *Hanging your quilt*, page 152. If you make tabs, you'll need to cut 5 strips of black fabric, 6x8½″ each.

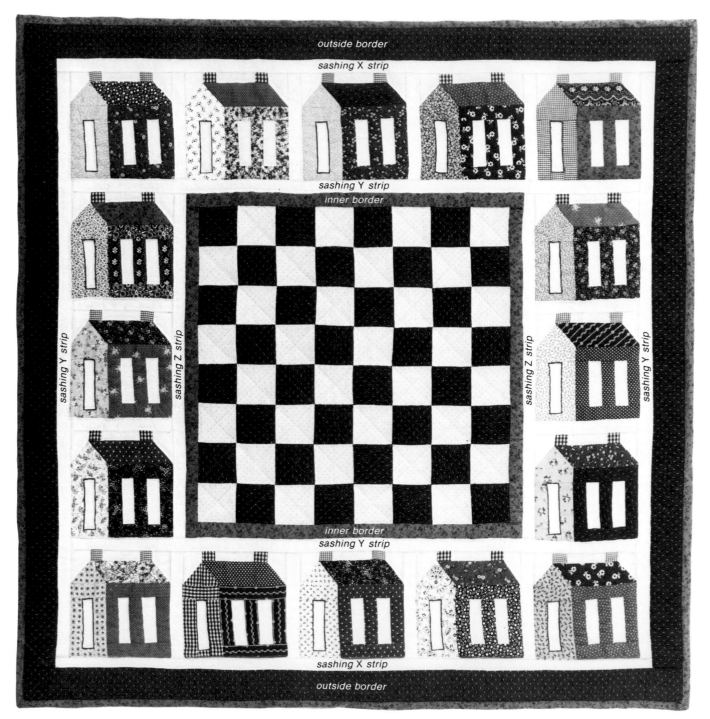

(color photo, page 85)

_____ *LET'S MAKE MORE PATCHWORK QUILTS*

10 Checkerboard and Schoolhouse Wall Hanging

Most one-room schoolhouses have disappeared from the countryside, but the schoolhouse quilt pattern is still popular. Here, I've combined it with a big checkerboard—another bit of nostalgia.

Half of the 16 schoolhouse blocks are done in rust or tan prints, with black print roofs. The other eight are in black or white prints, with rust roofs.

The black print checkerboard squares in the center match the outside border. For the second checkerboard fabric, I used an off-white print that I had on hand. To save buying extra yardage, you could substitute the off-white sashing fabric for these squares. There will be enough fabric left after you cut the long sashing strips.

The finished wall hanging is 52" square.

Materials

(Yardage is for fabric 45" wide.)

3½ yd. black print, for outside border, backing, checkerboard squares, 1 schoolhouse side and 1 roof
1½ yd. off-white solid, for sashing, windows, doors, sky (and for checkerboard squares, if you wish)
¾ yd. off-white print, for checkerboard squares (optional)
¾ yd. dark rust print, for inner border, bias binding, 1 schoolhouse side and 1 roof
¼ yd. (or 12" square) each of 7 black prints
¼ yd. (or 12" square) each of 7 dark rust prints
¼ yd. (or 9" square) each of 7 white with black prints
¼ yd. (or 9" square) each of 7 light rust or tan prints
¼ yd. black-and-white small check, for chimneys and 1 schoolhouse front
¼ yd. rust-and-white small check, for chimneys and 1 schoolhouse front
Thread for piecing in white or blending color
Quilting thread in white or colors
Black embroidery floss
1 pkg. polyester batting, 72x90"

Prepare fabric

Prewash all the fabric if you plan to wash the finished wall hanging. Then cut off sections which will be used later.

If you are going to use the off-white solid for the checkerboard squares, cut off a section 12x48" along the length, and set aside for the long sashing pieces.

From the dark rust border print, cut a 27" square, and set aside for bias binding.

From the black border print, cut an 18x54" section along the length. Use this section for piecing blocks; set aside remaining piece for outside border and backing.

Make blocks

For tips on making templates and piecing the blocks, see Chapter 1.

CHECKERBOARD

For this large center block use two fabrics—a black print and an off-white print or solid.

Make templates
Trace pattern for square A, page 146, and make a template.

Cut fabric
Place template A on the wrong side of the fabric and trace. Cut out, adding ¼" to ½" seam allowances:
   32 A squares of black print (same as border)
   32 A squares of off-white print or solid

Assemble
Pin-baste each black square to an off-white square and stitch together. If you use a machine, you can speed the work by stitching the pairs together in a long row, assembly-line fashion. Then snip the units apart. Trim each seam and finger-press seam allowances to the dark side.

Lay stitched units, face up, to form eight horizontal rows (see photo, opposite page). Join units in each row.

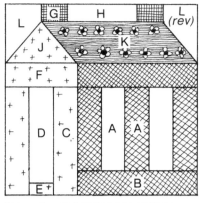

Fig. 1 *SCHOOLHOUSE*

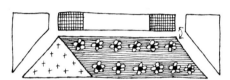

Fig. 2 *Piecing roof, chimneys and corner pieces*

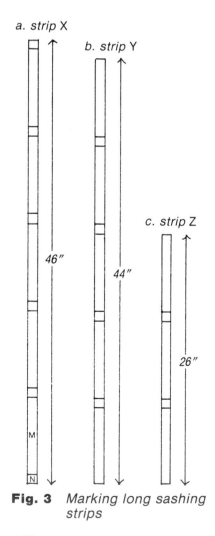

Fig. 3 *Marking long sashing strips*

Pin-baste the top two rows together, placing a pin wherever two seam lines meet. Then stitch the seam.

Continue adding a row at a time until the block is completed. Be careful to match all seam lines—we do want a nice, neat checkerboard!

SCHOOLHOUSE

A group of geometric shapes, mostly rectangles, forms the design in Fig. 1. You'll need 16 of these blocks, and each one has four different prints.

For each of eight blocks, select two rust or tan prints—a light one for the schoolhouse front, and a dark one for the side. Then add a black print roof and rust-and-white check chimneys.

For each of the other eight blocks, choose a white print for the schoolhouse front, and a black print for the side. Then add a dark rust roof and black-and-white check chimneys.

Make templates

Trace patterns A-N, page 146, and make a separate template for each piece. (There is no I pattern.) Patterns A-G and M-N are shown on one strip, 1" wide. For each pattern piece, measure from bottom of strip up to correct marking and trace. Pattern M, for sashing, is the full strip (1x8"). Label all templates.

Cut fabric

In the list below, sometimes two colors are given. Follow the first color when tracing pieces for eight blocks. Then follow the color in parenthesis when tracing pieces for eight more blocks.

For each block, lay templates on the wrong side of the fabric and trace. Cut out, adding ¼" to ½" seam allowances:

- 3 A rectangles of dark rust (or black) print
- 2 A rectangles of off-white solid
- 2 B rectangles of dark rust (or black) print
- 2 C rectangles of light rust (or white) print
- 1 D rectangle of off-white solid
- 1 E rectangle of light rust (or white) print
- 1 F rectangle of light rust (or white) print
- 2 G rectangles of rust-and-white (or black-and-white) check
- 1 H rectangle of off-white solid
- 1 J triangle of light rust (or white) print
- 1 K roof of dark rust (or black) print
- 1 L shape of off-white solid
- 1 L (reversed) of off-white solid

Assemble

Lay pieces, face up, to form the block in Fig. 1. Let's do this design in sections.

Pin-baste and stitch all the A rectangles together. Remember to trim each seam, and finger-press it to the dark side. Then add a B to the top and bottom. There—you have the side of one schoolhouse.

Now for the front unit. Stitch the E to the bottom of D (door). Add a C to each side and an F to the top.

Stitch the schoolhouse front unit to the side unit.

Add the J triangle to the K (roof). Add a G (chimney) to each end of the H. Then join these two units (Fig. 2).

Add L corner pieces (one is reversed) to ends of roof unit. Stitch these seams in two steps, like diamonds, beginning at the top left. Stitch the short seam to the end of the pencil line, then stop and backstitch; do not stitch into the seam allowance. Begin stitching again at the end of the adjoining seam (between L and J) and continue out to the raw edge.

Repeat step at other end of the block.

To outline door panel, use black floss and the chain stitch (page 9).

Now that you've conquered one schoolhouse, go ahead and piece 15 more. Remember to keep your colors grouped. Rust and tan schoolhouses have black roofs, and white and black schoolhouses have rust roofs.

Complete quilt top

After you've assembled the checkerboard center and 16 schoolhouse blocks, you're ready to add the sashing and borders.

Cut inner border and sashing strips
Find the dark rust border print and the off-white solid fabrics that you saved for these pieces.

Take the M template. To mark the inner border, place the template on the wrong side of the rust fabric and mark the lengths needed (you can slide the template along as you trace). Cut out, adding ¼″ to ½″ seam allowances:
    2 strips, 1x26″ each
    2 strips, 1x24″ each

To mark the long sashing X strips, use both the M and N templates. On the wrong side of the off-white solid (along the fabric length), first trace the 1″ square N. Then butt the 1x8″ M template against the square and trace it. Move and trace the two templates in this manner, until you have a 1x46″ length (Fig. 3, a). Mark 1 more strip in this manner, leaving room for seam allowances between them. The pencil cross marks on each strip will line up with the corners of the blocks when you assemble rows.

To mark the long sashing Y strips, again use both templates, but begin with the longer M piece. Then trace the N. Move and trace the templates until you have a 1x44″ strip (Fig. 3, b). Mark 3 more strips in the same way, leaving room for seam allowances between them.

To mark the long sashing Z strips, use the two templates in the same way, beginning with the M. Move and trace the templates until you have a 1x26″ strip (Fig. 3, c). Mark 1 more strip, leaving room for seam allowances.

To mark the short sashing strips, use the M template and trace 12 strips, leaving room for seam allowances.

Cut out all sashing strips, adding ¼″ to ½″ seam allowances.

Add inner border and sashing
Work with the rust inner border (see photo, page 136). Stitch the two side (1x24″) pieces to the checkerboard square, then add the top and bottom (1x26″) pieces.

Arrange the schoolhouse blocks in a pleasing color sequence, with five blocks along the top and bottom, and three blocks on each side. Place a 1x8″ sashing strip between blocks in each row, and stitch the row together.

Add a long sashing Z strip to the inside edge of each vertical row, matching your pencil cross marks to corners of blocks. Add a long sashing Y strip to the inside edge of the top and bottom rows.

Stitch the rows to the center section, first adding the vertical rows, then the top and bottom rows.

To add outside sashing strips to the center section, first stitch a long sashing Y strip to both sides. Then add a long sashing X strip to the top and bottom.

Cut and add outside border
Make a template 3″ wide and about 15″ long. Place it on the wrong side of the black print border fabric and mark the lengths needed. Cut out, adding ¼″ to ½″ seam allowances:
    2 strips, 3x52″ each
    2 strips, 3x46″ each
Add strips to the large center unit. First stitch a 3x46″ strip to

the two sides; then stitch a 3x52″ strip to the top and bottom.

The outside edges of the quilt are marked on the wrong side of each border section. To transfer these guidelines to the right side of the fabric, baste over the pencil lines.

Finish quilt

See *Quilting the whole top*, page 149. Piece the backing fabric to make a 54″ square. Press the completed top and the backing.

Mark quilting lines
On the center checkerboard square, use a yardstick to mark diagonal lines that crisscross on each square. All other quilting will be along seam lines.

Quilting guides
Stack the layers, smoothing quilt top over backing and batting. Baste the layers together.

Before you begin stitching, see *Making quilting stitches*, page 148.

On checkerboard, quilt diagonal lines you marked. Quilt checkerboard along outside edge, and quilt sashing around the inner border, ¼″ from seam lines.

On each schoolhouse, quilt inside the door and windows and around the whole shape, ¼″ from seam lines. Also quilt the outside sashing strips, ¼″ from the border.

Finish edges
Make bias from the 27″ square of rust print, and stitch bias to the quilt. Follow directions under *Using continuous bias*, page 151.

Add fabric for hanging
For this design, I prefer a hidden sleeve so that no additional fabric shows. Follow directions under *Add a sleeve*, page 152.

(color photo, page 120)

11

Stained Glass Roses Wall Hanging

One recent innovation in the world of quilting is the stained glass technique, and I think you may enjoy trying it. (At least your work won't break if you drop it.)

Black bias tape takes the place of leading, and it covers all lines in the design. Fabrics are in solid colors only—prints don't work as well.

In this design, each rose has three shades of yellow and three shades of orange. A black border frames the roses and is folded over the edge to the back. The finished wall hanging is 32" square.

Check your scrap bag before you buy fabric for the roses— you may have enough of some colors on hand. When combining colors, keep a few strips of black bias handy. Place these between the fabrics to judge the effect.

You can purchase the bias tape, but I like to make my own. It's easy. Just be sure you have all-cotton fabric so the folds you press along the bias edges will stay crisp.

Materials
(Yardage is for fabric 45" wide.)

¾ yd. aqua solid fabric, for background
⅔ yd. black solid (all cotton), for bias (*or* 7 pkg. black double-fold bias tape, 3 yd. each)
¾ yd. black solid, for border
¼ yd. each of 6 blending colors (light yellow, bright medium yellow, gold, light orange, medium orange and deep orange)
¼ yd. green solid, for leaves
1 yd. print or solid, for backing
1 pkg. polyester batting, 45x60"
Thread for appliqué in black
Black quilting thread
2 sheets of poster board, 22x28" each (cut and tape these together to make a 24" square)

Prepare fabric

Prewash and press all fabric if you plan to wash the finished wall hanging.

Make top

You must enlarge the pattern, page 142, before you can cut the rose and leaf appliqués.

Enlarge pattern
Use the 24" square of poster board. With a yardstick, draw a grid of vertical and horizontal lines, 1" apart.

Refer to the grid on the pattern, next page, and number the rows on your poster board grid to match.

With the numbers as a guide, use a pencil to copy the design from the book to your poster board. Work square by square (Fig. 1)—it's not difficult.

After you have drawn everything to your satisfaction, go over the lines with a black pen.

Draw design on fabric
Place the poster board design, face down, on the wrong side of the aqua fabric; keep edges on the straight grain. Tape poster board to fabric, and trace around the outside edges of the board to mark seam lines. With template still in place, cut out fabric, adding ¼" to ½" seam allowances.

Turn fabric over, and you should be able to see the design through the fabric. Lightly copy all the lines with a sharp No. 5H or 6H pencil.

Remove poster board from fabric; do not cut design apart.

Cut appliqué pieces
On the poster board, label the flower sections with the letters used on pattern. These will be your key to colors.

Each rose has six fabrics. When adjoining petals are the

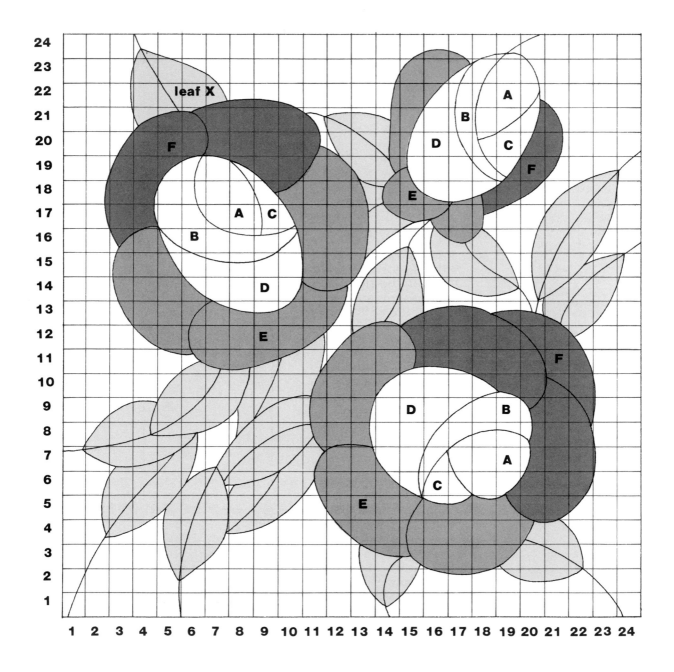

**Pattern for
STAINED GLASS ROSES
(to be enlarged)**

EACH SQUARE = 1 SQUARE INCH

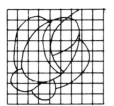

Fig. 1 *Enlarging pattern*

Fig. 2 *Cutting flower sections*

Fig. 3 *Cutting leaf sections*

Fig. 4 *Placing first bias strip*

same color, mark and cut them in one piece (Fig. 2).

Lay each color fabric, right side up, on top of the correct flower section and trace (you can see the design lines through the fabric). Cut out fabric, adding a scant ⅛″ seam allowance. (This must be kept narrow so it will be completely covered with bias.) For each flower you need:

    1 A of medium orange
    1 B of deep orange
    1 C of light orange
    1 D of bright medium
      yellow
    1 E of light yellow
    1 F of gold

Some of the leaves also can be cut in groups (Fig. 3).

If you can't see through the green fabric, use paper templates. Place typing-weight paper over the poster board and trace the leaf sections. Cut out the paper templates, place them on the right side of the green fabric and trace. Cut out fabric, adding scant ⅛″ seam allowances.

To draw veins and individual leaf shapes, cut your paper templates apart. Position templates on green fabric and trace needed lines.

Make bias (optional)

If you are going to make your own bias, the first step is to draft a poster board template ¾″ wide and about 10″ long.

From the black all-cotton fabric, cut a 24″ square. Then turn to page 151 and read *Using continuous bias.* Follow directions to cut the fabric square on the diagonal, join the edges, mark the strips (using your ¾″-wide template), make a tube and cut the long strip. You'll have about 20 yards of bias, all in one piece.

Lay one end of the bias on the ironing board. Fold one raw edge ¼″ to the center and press. Continue folding and pressing along the entire length of bias.

Next fold the opposite raw edge about ¼″, covering the

first raw edge, and press. Finished bias will be about ¼″ wide.

Position appliqué pieces

Place all the rose and leaf sections on the aqua background fabric, and pin. Pencil lines on appliqués should line up with pencil lines on the background. When two appliqué fabrics meet, seam allowances will overlap.

Baste edges of each appliqué piece in place, sewing along the pencil lines. This will hold overlapping edges together. Since all the basting will be covered with bias, it will not be removed, and the thread can be any color.

Add bias strips

If you made your own bias, use the strip flat. If you purchased double-fold bias, use it double—as it comes from the package. When you cut bias strips, try to avoid using the seams where bias is stitched together—these tend to form lumps in the "leading."

All raw edges of fabric are covered with bias strips. You'll have to plan ahead, and determine which strip should go on first and which should overlap.

Let's begin with leaf X in the upper left corner of the design. Cut a strip of bias just a little longer than needed to cover the first line (Fig. 4). Lay the bias in place, easing it on the curve; add pins perpendicular to the bias.

With black thread and the appliqué stitch (page 8), first sew along the inside curve (this keeps the bias smooth). Then sew along the outside curve.

Trim ends of bias, leaving ⅛″ beyond each end of the line being covered; bias will be cut on a slant in some cases.

Position next bias strip (Fig. 5, b) and pin in place. Sew along the inside curve, then the outside curve, and trim ends as for first strip (a).

Add last strip (c) in the same manner. This will cover cut

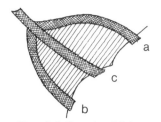

Fig. 5 *Adding last bias strip*

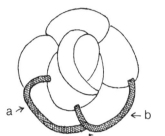

Fig. 6 *Adding bias to petals*

strip b covers
end of strip a

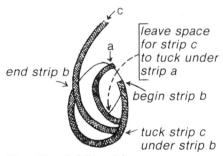

[leave space
for strip c
to tuck under
strip a]

end strip b

begin strip b

tuck strip c
under strip b

Fig. 7 *Adding bias
to center of rose*

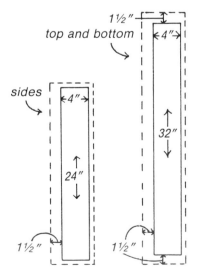

top and bottom

sides

1½"

4"

4"

32"

24"

1½"

1½"

Fig. 8 *Marking border pieces*

ends of strips (a) and (b), and continue on to the outside edge.

As a general rule, work with one strip of bias at a time. You may want to use several strips to help work out the layering in an area, but don't try to pin all the strips in place ahead of time. It will only confuse you.

Sew bias to the leaves first, then the roses.

When you begin the roses, work on the outer petals first (Fig. 6). Cut and sew the first strip (a). Begin at the center area of the flower and end at adjoining petal line, leaving ⅛" extra at both ends. Begin second strip (b) at center area and end at next petal line; this covers cut end of first strip.

In some cases, you'll find that you have to tuck an end of one strip under another strip as you sew (see Fig. 7 as an example). First, sew strip (a) in place, leaving a space on inside edge for strip (c) to tuck under later. Add strip (b), covering end of strip (a); tuck end of strip (c) under strip (b) and continue sewing. Sew strip (c) in place, curving around top of rose; finish with end of (c) tucked under strip (a).

Cut border pieces

Make a template 4" wide and about 12" long (you can slide the template along when marking fabric). Place the template on the wrong side of the black border fabric and mark the lengths needed.

For sides, mark 2 pieces, 4x24" each. Add 1½" for turning and seam allowance on one long (24") edge, and ¼" to ½" seam allowances on all other edges (Fig. 8).

For top and bottom, mark 2 pieces, 4x32" each. Add 1½" for turning and seam allowance on one long (32") edge and on each short edge, and add a ¼" to ½" seam allowance on the remaining long edge.

Cut out the four border pieces.

Add border

Pin and stitch border pieces to the center section, first adding the two sides and then the top and bottom.

To mark the turning line on border pieces, run a basting thread along the outside pencil lines. You will have 1½" of fabric extending beyond these lines.

Finish
wall hanging

See *Quilting the whole top,* page 149. From the backing fabric, cut a 32" square—the backing is the same size as the finished wall hanging.

Press the backing and the completed top. All quilting will be along the bias and seam lines, so there are no quilting lines to mark.

Stack the layers. Begin with backing, right side down. Add batting. Then center the appliquéd top, right side up. The top is wider and longer than the other layers; basting lines on border should be over cut edges of backing and batting. Baste the layers together.

Quilting guides

With black thread, quilt on both sides of all bias strips, ¼" from bias edges. (See *Making quilting stitches,* page 148.) Also quilt aqua background along outside edges, ¼" from seam lines.

On border, quilt along inside edges, ¼" from seam lines, and along outside edges, ¼" from basting lines.

Finish edges

Follow directions for *Folding border over edges,* page 151.

Add fabric for hanging

Follow directions under *Hanging your quilt,* page 152. If you make tabs, you'll need to cut 4 strips of black fabric, 6x8½" each.

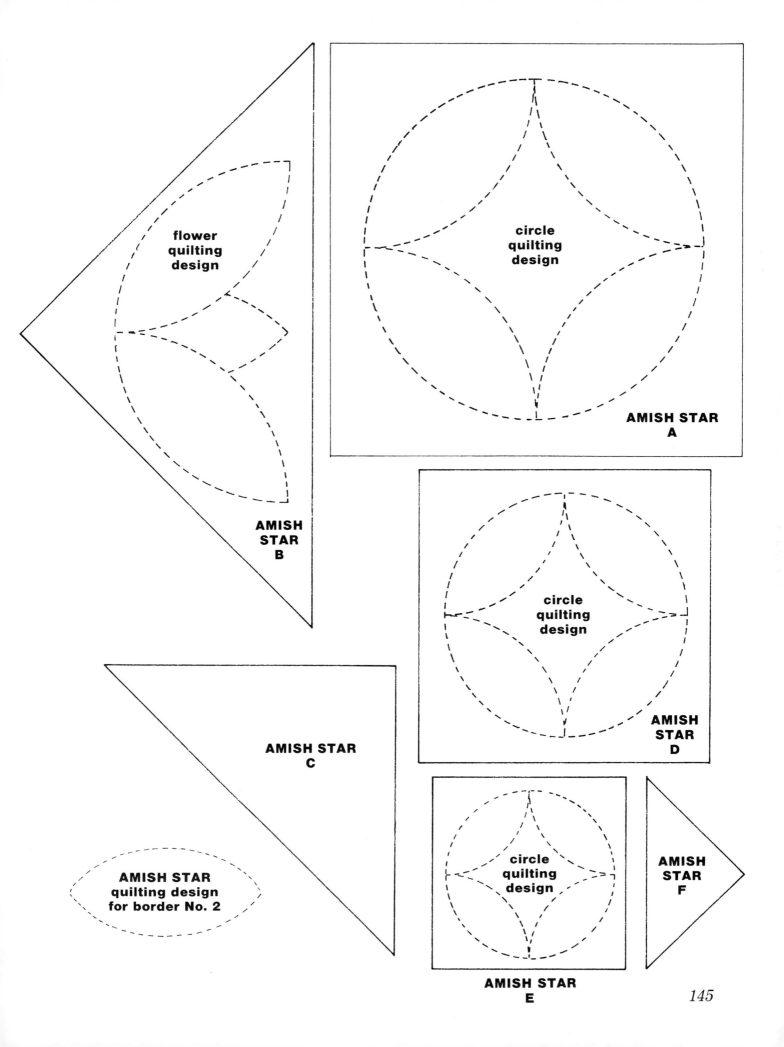

flower
quilting
design

AMISH
STAR
B

circle
quilting
design

**AMISH STAR
A**

circle
quilting
design

**AMISH
STAR
D**

**AMISH STAR
C**

AMISH STAR
quilting design
for border No. 2

circle
quilting
design

**AMISH
STAR
F**

**AMISH STAR
E**

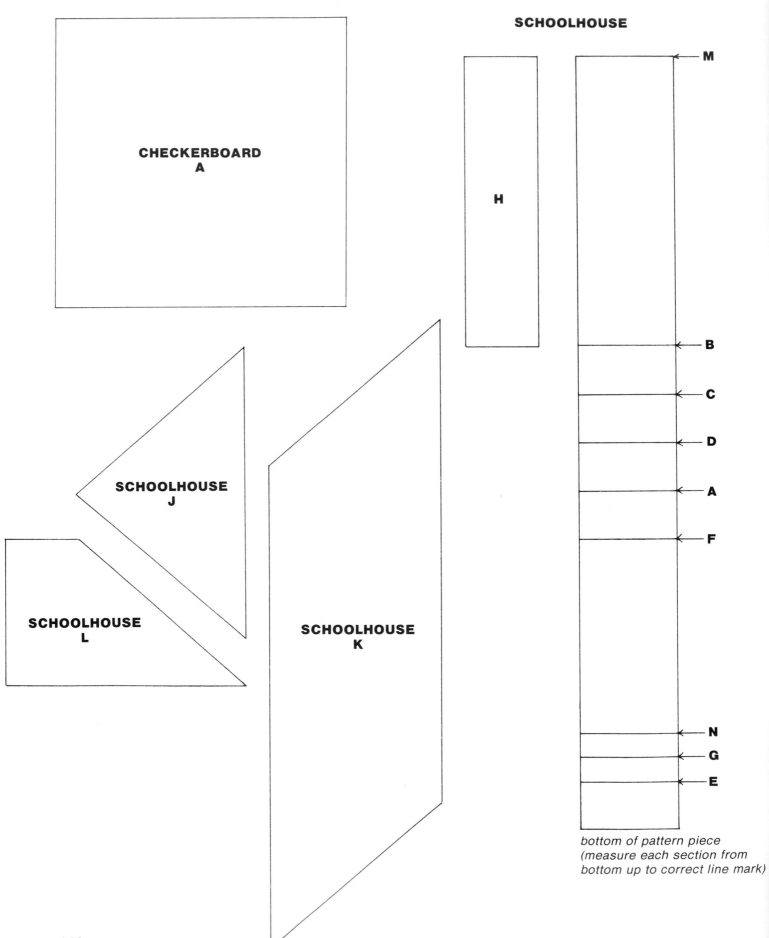

CHECKERBOARD
A

SCHOOLHOUSE

H

M

B

C

D

A

F

N

G

E

SCHOOLHOUSE
J

SCHOOLHOUSE
L

SCHOOLHOUSE
K

bottom of pattern piece
(measure each section from
bottom up to correct line mark)

12 Quilting and Finishing

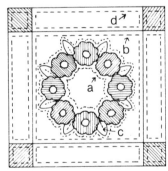

Fig. 1 *Quilting a pieced block and one-color sashing*

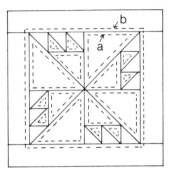

Fig. 2 *Quilting an appliqué block and two-color sashing*

Fig. 3 *Marking diagonal lines*

A finished quilt has three layers—a top, a filling of batting, and a backing. These layers are held together with quilting stitches.

Before you join the layers, you must decide how you will do the quilting. One method is to assemble the whole top and then quilt it (see *Quilting the whole top*, page 149). The method can be used for any project in this book, and it's the only one to follow for the crib quilts, wall hangings and the large Glittering Star quilt.

The second method—quilting in sections—is an alternate choice for all the other large quilts. With this method, you assemble sections, quilt them, then stitch them together (see *Quilting in sections*, page 150).

Deciding on quilting lines

Most quilting follows a seam, so you have a guide for your stitches. For other lines, such as diagonals or swirls, you'll have to mark the quilt top.

Basic quilting

As a general rule, you can quilt pieced work ¼″ from seam lines (Fig. 1, a). Quilt inside each shape—or selected shapes. For example, on a block with many triangles, you may choose to quilt every other one. On a narrow sashing or

border strip, you may decide to quilt along only one edge.

On appliqués (Fig. 2), quilt around the shapes (a) and along the inside edges of the background square (b), ¼″ from the seam lines. You also can quilt inside an appliqué to help define a design, like the center of a leaf (c).

If all the sashing is the same color, quilt around the blocks, ¼″ from seam lines (Fig. 1, b). If the sashing has corner squares in a contrasting color, quilt inside each piece, ¼″ from the seam lines (Fig. 2, d).

Marking simple lines and shapes

To mark diagonal lines for quilting (Fig. 3), use a yardstick. Draw the first line from corner to corner, then place additional lines, measuring equal spaces in between.

To mark an outline for a shape, such as a heart (Fig. 4) or a leaf, you can cut a template from poster board or plastic and position it on the quilt top for tracing. For a simple inside line, such as a leaf vein, you can mark it by eye or cut the template apart along the design line for tracing.

On light-colored fabric, mark lines with a No. 5H or 6H pencil. *On dark fabric*, use a white, yellow or silver drawing pencil, or even a sliver of soap.

If you'd rather not mark the fabric (or have trouble seeing the lines), there are some alter-

Fig. 4 *Tracing heart shape*

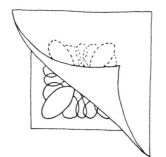

Fig. 5 *Marking swirl design on light-colored fabric*

natives. To outline shapes, cut a template from nonwoven interfacing, pin it in place and quilt around it. For straight lines, position masking tape on fabric and quilt along the edge.

On the Wedding Sampler quilt, I used a heart template cut from interfacing to quilt along the border, and I used masking tape to quilt diagonal lines in the center panel.

Marking special designs

To copy more intricate quilting designs, such as a swirl pattern (Fig. 5), first trace the complete design onto tracing paper or any other paper you can see through.

For light-colored fabric, transfer the design to a piece of poster board, using carbon paper under the tracing. Remove the tracing and carbon paper and go over lines on the poster board with a felt-tip pen. Position the poster board drawing under the fabric and tape or pin it in place. Trace design lightly onto the fabric with a No. 5H or 6H pencil.

For dark fabric, position the tracing itself on top of the fabric. Slip a sheet of white or yellow dressmaker's carbon between the layers and retrace the design with a dry ball-point pen (one with no ink). *Note:* Don't press the fabric with an iron after you've marked it with dressmaker's carbon or the lines will disappear.

Making quilting stitches

Quilting thread is strong, so your pretty quilting stitches won't break. It comes in many colors, and you can match the quilt fabrics or use contrasting colors. Many traditional quilters use only white thread. The choice is yours.

Quilting needles, also called Betweens, are short and easy to thread. You might start with a size 8 and graduate to a smaller size 10. These short

needles really do help you take short stitches.

Thread the needle with about 18″ of single thread and make a small knot in one end. Insert the needle in the top of the quilt layers, about an inch from where you want to start quilting. Go through the batting only and bring the needle up on the quilting line. With a little tug, pull the knot through the top fabric and into the batting where it won't show.

The quilting stitch is a small, even running stitch (page 4). Work as evenly as you can. Make stitches and spaces the same length, and be sure every stitch goes through all layers. (You'll have to put one hand under the work and use your fingers to feel the needle as it comes through—so be prepared for grazed fingers.) Try to make 6 to 8 stitches per inch on the top layer. Practice, and eventually you'll have it.

Begin quilting in the middle of the quilt top or section, and work outward to avoid forming lumps. To move from one area to another, slide the needle and thread through the batting and come up on the next line of quilting.

When you have used most of the thread, you have several ways of securing it. One way is to end as you began—by burying a knot in the batting. To do this, make a knot close to the fabric (near the last stitch). Take one last stitch into the batting only (don't catch the backing fabric), bringing the needle up about an inch away from the stitching line. Tug the thread to pull the knot into the batting, then clip the thread close to the fabric.

Another way to secure the thread is limited to work you can turn over easily, such as crib quilts and separate sections of a large quilt. First, take a final stitch on the right side and pull the needle through to the back. Turn the work over so the backing fabric is up, and begin working back into the

Fig. 6 *Securing thread with backstitches*

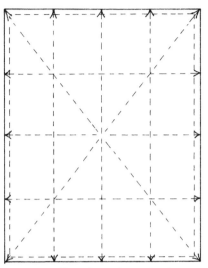

Fig. 7 *Basting the whole top before quilting*

line of quilting (Fig. 6). Take one backstitch into the backing (do not catch the top fabric), and bring the needle up to the *left* of stitch (a). Take a backstitch over (a) so it will look like a single stitch when finished; go into the batting and come up to the left of stitch (b). Backstitch over (b), then wiggle the needle through the batting for about an inch in a different direction. Bring the needle up, and clip the thread close to the fabric.

Quilting the whole top

Complete the top layer, following directions for your individual quilt, and press.

Plan your quilting and mark any lines or designs you'll need. (See *Deciding on quilting lines*, page 147.)

Cut backing fabric, piecing if necessary, and press.

Stack layers

Clear floor space where you can work on a large rug or carpet. Lay the backing piece, right side down, and pin or tape it to the rug.

Unroll batting and pat it in place on top of the backing. It should be the same size. If the batting is too big, trim it. If it's not big enough, take another roll and butt the edge against the first batt. Join edges with long, loose stitches.

Add the quilt top, right side up, and smooth it out carefully. If bias will be used to finish the edges, the backing and batting layers should extend 1″ beyond the top on all sides.

If the border will be folded to the back as a finish, the top will be larger than the other layers. Keep the basting lines on the top even with the edges of the backing and batting.

Pin through layers with T-pins, anchoring pins in the rug.

Baste the layers

Some people crawl around on the floor to baste the layers together. (Maybe a few friends will help with a large quilt.) Other people pin layers together with many large safety pins, then carefully transfer the unit to a table for basting.

No matter where you baste, use white thread and keep all knots on top. Begin each basting line in the center of the quilt. First sew from the center to the middle of each edge, then from center to each corner. Baste around the edge of the quilt.

Finally, add horizontal and vertical lines (Fig.7); there should be no open space larger than 6″. You will have a nice, firm package to handle.

Do the quilting

For a large quilt like the Glittering Star, you must use a quilting frame or hoop. Otherwise, it's impossible to keep the layers smooth and in position. Also, there's too much fabric and batting to roll up and hold in your hand. With a quilting frame or hoop, you'll have to use a thimble to push the needle through the layers.

For smaller pieces such as wall hangings and crib quilts, you can use a hoop or not. I prefer to quilt without one.

Before you begin quilting, see *Making quilting stitches*, page 148.

When you've completed the quilting, you're ready to cover the edges. (See *Finishing the edges*, page 151.)

If you plan to use your quilt as a wall hanging, see *Hanging your quilt*, page 152.

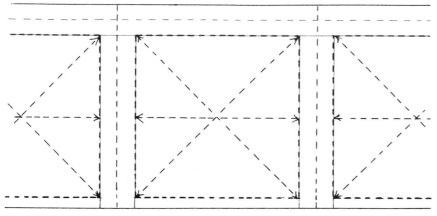

Fig. 8 *Basting a section before quilting*

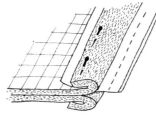

Fig. 9 *Joining quilted sections*

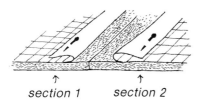

section 1   section 2

Fig. 10 *Trimming batting so edges butt together*

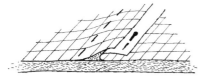

Fig. 11 *Preparing to quilt seam area*

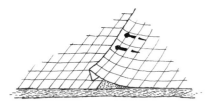

Fig. 12 *Pinning backing for hemming*

Quilting in sections

I use this method for large quilts whenever possible because I find sections easier to baste, stitch and carry around than whole quilts. Obviously, you can use this method only with quilts that can be easily divided into units.

You'll need extra backing fabric and batting for quilting in sections, and I've noted this under fabric requirements for the individual quilts.

First complete the quilt top sections (rows, border pieces or other units), according to directions for the individual quilt. Press each section.

Plan the quilting, and mark any lines or designs you'll need. (See *Deciding on quilting lines,* page 147.)

Work with one section at a time. Measure the finished section, then cut the backing fabric 2″ wider and longer. Press the backing.

Stack the layers

Place the backing fabric, right side down, on the floor. Over this, smooth a layer of batting, cut the same size. Then add the quilt top section, right side up; let the backing and batting extend 1″ beyond the top layer on all sides.

Pin the layers together, then pick up the section and place it on a table for basting.

Baste the layers

Begin at the center of the section. Use white thread and keep the knots on top. Baste each block or unit from the center to the middle of each edge, and then from the center to each corner (Fig. 8). Baste around the block on top of the seam lines. Repeat steps to baste other blocks in the row, working evenly away from the center block. Finally, if there are sashing strips, baste along the center of each strip.

On border sections, baste down the middle of the border, from the center to each end. Add rows of stitches across the short width to create a grid, with lines about 6″ apart. Always work from the center to the outside.

Do the quilting

You can use a quilting hoop or not. I like to quilt without one so that I can manipulate the fabric. (Try working without a hoop if you don't like to wear a thimble.)

Before you begin quilting, see *Making quilting stitches,* page 148. Start at the center of each section and work evenly toward the edges, keeping the layers smooth.

One thing you must remember in section quilting: Stop quilting about an inch away from any raw edge that will be stitched to another section. This keeps the seam allowances free. You will complete quilting along edges after seams are stitched.

Join the sections

When two adjacent sections are quilted, such as the first two rows of a quilt, remove all basting threads. Pin the batting and backing fabric away from the edges to be joined.

Pin edges of the sections with right sides together, matching all intersecting seam lines. Sew the two sections together (Fig. 9). Trim the seam allowances to ¼″ and finger-press to one side.

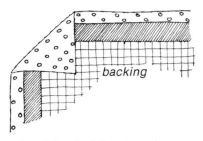

Fig. 13 *Folding border to begin miter*

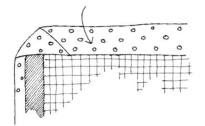

Fig. 14 *Folding first edge to back*

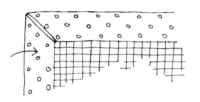

Fig. 15 *Folding second edge to back*

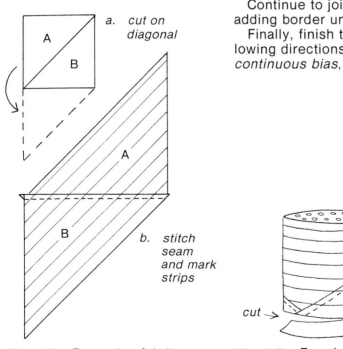

a. *cut on diagonal*

b. *stitch seam and mark strips*

Fig. 16 *Preparing fabric for bias*

cut →

Fig. 17 *Forming tube of bias*

Lay joined sections flat on a table, with backing side up. Trim batting so edges butt together (Fig. 10). To do this, release batting on the first section (keep backing pinned out of the way). Smooth the batting and let it extend ¼″ beyond the seam you just stitched; trim if necessary.

Then release batting on second section, smooth and trim so that it butts against the first section.

Unpin backing on first section, smooth over batting, and baste in place (Fig. 11). Turn work over and complete the quilting on the first section. (If you are quilting without a hoop, and there seems to be a lot of bulk under your hand, roll the section so that you can get to the quilting area.)

Remove basting. Trim backing on first section, leaving about ¼″ beyond the quilting stitches.

Release backing fabric on the second section and smooth over first section. Baste in place and complete quilting. Turn raw edge under ½″ and pin to first section (Fig. 12). Sew along the folded edge, using the appliqué stitch (page 8).

Continue to join the sections, adding border units last.

Finally, finish the edges, following directions under *Using continuous bias*, next column.

Finishing the edges

By this time, your work is quilted and you have only the edges left to finish.

I've used two methods for the quilts in this book. Two crib quilts and the Stained Glass Roses wall hanging are finished by folding the border over the edges and sewing it to the backing. All other quilts and wall hangings are finished with continuous strips of bias.

Folding border over edges

Backing fabric and batting are cut the same size as the finished quilt. If these have "grown" a bit during quilting (batting usually does), trim them to line up with the basting stitches on the quilt top.

Turn the border edges ½″ to the wrong side and press. Miter each corner, following these steps: Fold the border in a diagonal across the corner, with corner of backing at the fold line (Fig. 13). Fold one edge of the border to the back along the basting line (Fig. 14). Fold next border edge to back along basting line (Fig. 15).

Hand-stitch mitered edges together, and hand-stitch border edges to the backing.

Using continuous bias

Making continuous bias is like a magic trick.

Begin with a square of fabric, using dimensions given for your quilt. Cut square in half on the diagonal (Fig. 16, a), then sew top section to bottom section. Stitch with right sides together, using a ¼″ seam. Press seam to one side.

Make a template 2½″ wide and at least 10″ long. Beginning at one bias edge, mark 2½″ widths (Fig. 16, b). Bring the two straight-grain edges together to form a tube, with right side inside; let one full bias width extend beyond the tube at one end, as in Fig. 17. Match pencil lines ¼″ from the edge (where seam will be stitched), and stitch the seam.

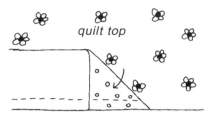

Fig. 18 *Adding bias to quilt*

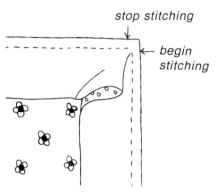

Fig. 19 *Forming a mitered corner*

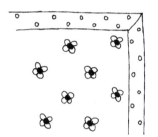

Fig. 20 *Mitered corner after turning*

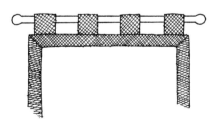

Fig. 21 *Adding tabs for wall hanging*

Start with the extension at one end, and cut along the pencil line until you have one continuous strip of bias. There—didn't that seem like magic?

Check the quilt to be sure all outside edges are even and straight. Trim excess batting and backing to line up with the quilt top.

Fold down one end of the bias to make a triangle (Fig. 18). Place this end on the quilt, along the bottom edge at center. Have right sides together, and keep edge of bias even with edge of quilt. (When the bias triangle is finally covered with the other end of the strip, the fold will look like a diagonal seam.)

Instead of pinning the bias all the way around, I like to hold it in place as I work. Machine-stitch ½" from the edge.

When you come to a corner, you can ease the bias around it, or you can miter it as I do.

To miter a corner, refer to Fig. 19 and follow these steps: Stop stitching ½" from the corner. Take the bias out to the corner and turn it to go down the adjacent edge, creating a fold in the bias strip. Begin stitching the next side ½" from the corner (do not catch the corner fold).

Continue adding bias, handling all four corners of the quilt in the same way.

When you come to the bottom edge, end by overlapping the triangular fold you made at the beginning. Cut off any extra length of bias.

Fold the bias over the quilt edge. On mitered corners, each corner fold will automatically form a miter on the front (Fig. 20); arrange fold on back to form an even miter there, too. Sew the mitered folds by hand.

Turn raw edges of bias under ½" and sew folded edge to backing by hand; use the appliqué stitch (page 8).

Now your work is bound and beautiful. What a feeling of accomplishment you should have!

Hanging your quilt

All quilts that you want to hang should have a special fabric holder to use with a rod. Never, never tack a quilt directly to the wall.

Add a sleeve

This can be used for any size quilt, but it's the only way to hang a large one. A sleeve distributes the weight evenly.

The sleeve won't show, so you can use plain muslin. Cut a strip of fabric as long as the top of the quilt and 4½" wide. Fold all raw edges ¼" to the wrong side and press. Then machine-stitch along each short end.

Pin the flat strip to the back of the quilt, just below the top edge. Hand-stitch sleeve to quilt along both long edges.

Slip rod through the sleeve to hang quilt. Select a rod and brackets that are sturdy enough to support the weight of the quilt. For a large quilt, I like a wooden rod that is 1" in diameter.

Add tabs

Another way to hang a small quilt is to add fabric tabs to the top edge (Fig. 21). These tabs will show, so you'll want to use a fabric that matches part of the quilt, probably the binding or the border.

To make each tab, cut a strip of fabric 6x8½". Fold in half lengthwise with right side inside. Stitch a ¼" lengthwise seam, turn right side out, and press with seam centered on the back.

Turn raw edges ¼" to the inside of tube and press. Fold tab in half to make it 2¾x4".

Pin tabs along the top edge. Place one at each end, then space other tabs evenly in between. Try to leave no more than 8" between them. Sew tabs in place.

Slip rod through the tabs to hang quilt.

Index

Page numbers for color photos are in boldface type